Echo Quick Start Guide

Build lightweight and high-performance web apps with Echo

J. Ben Huson

BIRMINGHAM - MUMBAI

Echo Quick Start Guide

Copyright © 2018 Packt Publishing

All rights reserved. No part of this book may be reproduced, stored in a retrieval system, or transmitted in any form or by any means, without the prior written permission of the publisher, except in the case of brief quotations embedded in critical articles or reviews.

Every effort has been made in the preparation of this book to ensure the accuracy of the information presented. However, the information contained in this book is sold without warranty, either express or implied. Neither the author, nor Packt Publishing or its dealers and distributors, will be held liable for any damages caused or alleged to have been caused directly or indirectly by this book.

Packt Publishing has endeavored to provide trademark information about all of the companies and products mentioned in this book by the appropriate use of capitals. However, Packt Publishing cannot guarantee the accuracy of this information.

Commissioning Editor: Kunal Chaudhari
Acquisition Editor: Noyonika Das
Content Development Editor: Mohammed Yusuf Imaratwale
Technical Editor: Shweta Jadhav
Copy Editor: Safis Editing
Project Coordinator: Hardik Bhinde
Proofreader: Safis Editing
Indexer: Tejal Daruwale Soni
Graphics: Jason Monteiro
Production Coordinator: Nilesh Mohite

First published: May 2018

Production reference: 1280518

Published by Packt Publishing Ltd.
Livery Place
35 Livery Street
Birmingham
B3 2PB, UK.

ISBN 978-1-78913-943-3

www.packtpub.com

To my dearest wife, for her constant sacrifice and daily drudgery allow me to pursue my aspirations. To my dearest daughter, for her youthful curiosity inspires me to learn more and drive for a deeper understanding. To my Mom and Dad, for their guidance throughout my life has been key to my personal and professional success.

– J. Ben Huson

mapt.io

Mapt is an online digital library that gives you full access to over 5,000 books and videos, as well as industry leading tools to help you plan your personal development and advance your career. For more information, please visit our website.

Why subscribe?

- Spend less time learning and more time coding with practical eBooks and Videos from over 4,000 industry professionals
- Improve your learning with Skill Plans built especially for you
- Get a free eBook or video every month
- Mapt is fully searchable
- Copy and paste, print, and bookmark content

PacktPub.com

Did you know that Packt offers eBook versions of every book published, with PDF and ePub files available? You can upgrade to the eBook version at www.PacktPub.com and as a print book customer, you are entitled to a discount on the eBook copy. Get in touch with us at service@packtpub.com for more details.

At www.PacktPub.com, you can also read a collection of free technical articles, sign up for a range of free newsletters, and receive exclusive discounts and offers on Packt books and eBooks.

Contributors

About the author

J. Ben Huson is a senior engineer for a metrics and data analytics company. Ben's experience with web development began over 12 years ago and has constantly evolved with the technical landscape of the industry over that time. Ben enjoys working with and contributing to open source software, including the Echo web framework. Ben has contributed to and developed open source software solutions that are currently used in production services. Ben is currently finishing his MS in Computer Science.

About the reviewers

Aaron Torres received his master's of science degree in computer science from New Mexico Institute of Mining and Technology. He has worked on distributed systems in high-performance computing and in large-scale web and microservices applications.

Aaron has published a number of papers and has several patents in the areas of storage and I/O. He is passionate about sharing his knowledge and ideas with others. He is also a fan of the Go language and open source for backend systems and development.

Vishal Rana is the creator of the Echo web framework and many other popular open source projects. Currently, he is working as a staff engineer for PayPal, where he is involved in building distributed and scalable systems to process millions of events per day using Go, REST, Java, Docker, microservices, Hadoop, Kafka, Spark, Elasticsearch, and other open source technologies.

Packt is searching for authors like you

If you're interested in becoming an author for Packt, please visit `authors.packtpub.com` and apply today. We have worked with thousands of developers and tech professionals, just like you, to help them share their insight with the global tech community. You can make a general application, apply for a specific hot topic that we are recruiting an author for, or submit your own idea.

Table of Contents

Preface   1

Chapter 1: Understanding HTTP, Go, and Echo   7
   Technical requirements   8
   HTTP basics   8
      HTTP request   8
      HTTP response   11
   Go HTTP handlers   12
   Go HTTP web server   13
   Reasons for a framework   14
   Setting up the environment   14
   Setting up Echo   16
   Summary   18

Chapter 2: Developing Echo Projects   19
   Technical requirements   20
   Setting up a project in echo and organizing code   20
      Implementing a project   24
      Dependency management   26
   Routing and handlers   27
      Routing   28
      Handlers   28
   Middleware   31
      Custom middleware   32
   Rendering   32
   Summary   34

Chapter 3: Exploring Routing Capabilities   35
   Technical requirements   36
   Basic handler routing   36
      Adding routes   36
      How Echo routing works   38
   Group routing   40
   Router implementation considerations   42
   In action   44
   Summary   47

Chapter 4: Implementing Middleware   49
   Technical requirements   50

Basics of middleware processing	50
Middleware chaining	53
Creating custom middleware	57
In action	59
Summary	61

Chapter 5: Utilizing the Request Context and Data Bindings — 63
- **Technical requirements** — 64
- **Maintaining context** — 64
  - Globally requesting context mapping — 65
  - The new handler function type — 66
  - Hiding context within a request — 67
  - Post Go 1.7 — 68
  - Echo context — 68
- **Request binding** — 70
- **Response rendering** — 75
  - echo.Response — 76
- **Summary** — 78

Chapter 6: Performing Logging and Error Handling — 79
- **Technical requirements** — 80
- **Logging** — 80
  - Echo's Logger interface — 80
  - Log levels — 83
  - Logger middleware — 84
- **Error handling** — 85
  - Handling application panics — 87
- **Summary** — 88

Chapter 7: Testing Applications — 89
- **Technical requirements** — 90
- **Types of testing** — 90
  - Unit testing — 90
  - Benchmark testing — 90
  - Behavior testing — 91
  - Integration testing — 91
  - Security testing — 91
- **Unit testing middleware and handler code** — 91
- **Benchmark testing web applications** — 97
- **External behavior and integration testing** — 98
- **Summary** — 102

Chapter 8: Providing Templates and Static Content — 103
- **Technical requirements** — 104
- **Serving static files** — 104

Template basics	106
Templates within Echo	111
Calling Echo from templates	114
Summary	117
Other Books You May Enjoy	119
Index	123

Preface

This tour of web application development aims to express the capabilities required of a development framework, and also considers what is truly important for developer efficiency within the field of web application development. Starting with the basics of HTTP and progressing through the built-in features of Echo, we explore together how best to create, organize, and maintain a successful web application.

The plethora of Go web application frameworks currently in the wild is staggering, causing even experienced web application developers paralysis of analysis. Each web application framework out there has been subtly optimized for the particular use cases of the group of authors contributing to it. There are so many opinionated options out there that developers often choose one framework for their applications and figure out that the features of the framework do not align with the developer. Oftentimes, the lack of feature functionality or performance are limiting factors as well for adoption of a web application framework.

This book focuses on general web application development concepts framed within the Echo framework. We start by exploring general HTTP concepts and move onto how these concepts are fulfilled by the built-in features of Echo. In addition, this book explores exactly how Echo achieves performance and functional goals by diving deep into the particulars of how the features are implemented. This book aims to give a clear representation of the essential functionalities and features within Echo in order to provide developers not only with reasons to choose Echo, but to provide real examples of Echo in action, demonstrating how developer efficiency is improved.

Within this book, you will learn about the internal concepts of handler routing, middleware chaining, and maintaining context. We will demonstrate how you as a developer will increase efficiency through interacting with Echo for request binding and response rendering. You will be shown how to effectively log and handle errors, as well as how to create unit tests for your application. By looking at the essentials of the Echo framework, you will be equipped to make a positive impact in your development team.

 This book is referenced as Echo Essentials in the GitHub repository and code videos.

Who this book is for

Software developers who are fairly new to Go and are looking to employ a high-performance web application or backend API will be most rewarded by this book. Developers who have a performance requirement for their APIs and developers who have some Go experience, as well as experience with web application frameworks in general but not with Echo, will also benefit.

We assume that the reader will be well-versed in web technologies, with a basic understanding of the HTTP protocol and REST API design concepts. We further assume that the reader will have worked with another backend web application framework before and understands the processing pipelines that are common in web frameworks.

What this book covers

Chapter 1, *Understanding HTTP, Go, and Echo*, covers a high-level understanding of HTTP, Go, and the Echo framework. We explain how the Go HTTP standard library is structured and what useful primitives are included. By reviewing what features the standard library contains for HTTP requests, responses, and handling of requests, how using a web framework can improve the quality and robustness of your application will be evident. Also covered are some of the internals of the standard library web server and comparisons with Echo. Finally, we also cover initial environment setup in order for the reader to become immediately productive.

Chapter 2, *Exploring Routing Capabilities*, dives into a very fast and high-level tour of the major functionality of the Echo framework, and discusses around an optimal Echo project setup. Starting with the most basic Echo handler and working through an example application, we show the features and capabilities of Echo very briefly.

Chapter 3, *Implementing Middleware*, discusses one of the most common problems in web application development, which is how to appropriately map the resource described in the URL path to the actual code that represents the resource. Within this chapter, we will explain how Echo's routing engine works and provide real examples of how the routing capabilities within Echo perform better than other web frameworks in the space.

Chapter 4, *Developing Echo Projects*, covers request and response processing pipelines within Echo. By using middleware, we show how you can simplify your handler code by breaking handler units of work into middleware functions. We also explain how middleware chaining works and what to expect when you use middleware in Echo.

Chapter 5, *Utilizing the Request Context and Data Bindings*, explains how context is used within the Echo framework. Context within the Echo framework allows for simplification of otherwise difficult information passing. Since context is built into the handler function signature, your code will always have access to this construct. This chapter also investigates a few mechanisms related to the context, which are request binding and response rendering. The chapter shows examples of how to accomplish as well as some related best practices.

Chapter 6, *Performing Logging and Error Handling*, exposes to the reader an often-overlooked but critically important aspect of application design: logging and error handling. This chapter provides real examples of how logging and error handling can work within your Echo-based web applications.

Chapter 7, *Testing Applications*, marches into effective testing techniques for testing a web application API. We will start with some definitions of various forms of testing and then progress into test implementations. There are also neat tricks shown within the chapter to provide you with more information about coverage numbers from external testing.

Chapter 8, *Providing Templates and Static Content*, goes over how to interact with Echo's file serving capabilities in order to provide static content to your callers. By building on Go's html/template package, we also go into depth on how to make the most of dynamic template rendering.

To get the most out of this book

- An intermediate knowledge of the Go programming language as well as initial exposure to web application frameworks
- Ability to develop with an IDE and cursory experience on the command line

Download the example code files

You can download the example code files for this book from your account at www.packtpub.com. If you purchased this book elsewhere, you can visit www.packtpub.com/support and register to have the files emailed directly to you.

You can download the code files by following these steps:

1. Log in or register at www.packtpub.com.
2. Select the **SUPPORT** tab.
3. Click on **Code Downloads & Errata**.
4. Enter the name of the book in the **Search** box and follow the onscreen instructions.

Once the file is downloaded, please make sure that you unzip or extract the folder using the latest version of:

- WinRAR/7-Zip for Windows
- Zipeg/iZip/UnRarX for Mac
- 7-Zip/PeaZip for Linux

The code bundle for the book is also hosted on GitHub at https://github.com/PacktPublishing/Echo-Essentials. In case there's an update to the code, it will be updated on the existing GitHub repository.

We also have other code bundles from our rich catalog of books and videos available at https://github.com/PacktPublishing/. Check them out!

Download the color images

We also provide a PDF file that has color images of the screenshots/diagrams used in this book. You can download it here: http://www.packtpub.com/sites/default/files/downloads/EchoQuickStartGuide_ColorImages.pdf.

Code in Action

Visit the following link to check out videos of the code being run:
https://goo.gl/69xxFt

Conventions used

There are a number of text conventions used throughout this book.

`CodeInText`: Indicates code words in text, database table names, folder names, filenames, file extensions, pathnames, dummy URLs, user input, and Twitter handles. Here is an example: "The parameters include two string arguments, method and path, as well as an `echo.HandlerFunc` variable for which the resulting request routing match should map."

A block of code is set as follows:

```
func (e *Echo) Add(method, path string, handler HandlerFunc, middleware
 ...MiddlewareFunc) *Route {
```

Any command-line input or output is written as follows:

```
mkdir -p $GOPATH/src/github.com/PacktPublishing

git clone https://github.com/PacktPublishing/Echo-Essentials
```

Bold: Indicates a new term, an important word, or words that you see onscreen. For example, words in menus or dialog boxes appear in the text like this. Here is an example: "Select **System info** from the **Administration** panel."

Warnings or important notes appear like this.

Tips and tricks appear like this.

Get in touch

Feedback from our readers is always welcome.

General feedback: Email `feedback@packtpub.com` and mention the book title in the subject of your message. If you have questions about any aspect of this book, please email us at `questions@packtpub.com`.

Errata: Although we have taken every care to ensure the accuracy of our content, mistakes do happen. If you have found a mistake in this book, we would be grateful if you would report this to us. Please visit www.packtpub.com/submit-errata, selecting your book, clicking on the Errata Submission Form link, and entering the details.

Piracy: If you come across any illegal copies of our works in any form on the Internet, we would be grateful if you would provide us with the location address or website name. Please contact us at copyright@packtpub.com with a link to the material.

If you are interested in becoming an author: If there is a topic that you have expertise in and you are interested in either writing or contributing to a book, please visit authors.packtpub.com.

Reviews

Please leave a review. Once you have read and used this book, why not leave a review on the site that you purchased it from? Potential readers can then see and use your unbiased opinion to make purchase decisions, we at Packt can understand what you think about our products, and our authors can see your feedback on their book. Thank you!

For more information about Packt, please visit packtpub.com.

Understanding HTTP, Go, and Echo

Echo is a performance-focused, open source Go web application framework. Go is an increasingly popular language choice for creating web applications due to the flexibility and performance built into the `net/http` standard library package that comes with the language. The `net/http` package provides many useful and powerful primitives, such as its web server implementation, request and response types and methods, uniform resource location router, as well as a clean handler interface and function type declaration.

We will begin by taking an inventory of the basic building blocks of a web application from the protocol. Then, we will explore what the `net/http` package provides, and very briefly touch on how a web application framework could build with these primitives to provide developers with structure for building successful applications. It will be shown how the Echo web application framework fills the voids left by the `net/http` package, allowing for ease of development. Finally, we will end with best practices for setting up your web application using Echo.

Within this chapter, we will cover:

- A refresher of the primitives of the **Hypertext Transport Protocol** (HTTP)
- An overview of what the `net/http` standard library provides
- A brief explanation of why the standard library is lacking and in need of a framework
- How to set up your Go environment and install the Echo Framework

Technical requirements

You will be required to know Go programming language, also basics of web application framework. You will also need to install Git, in order use the Git repository of this book. And finally, ability to develop with an IDE on the command line.

The code files of this chapter can be found on GitHub:
https://github.com/PacktPublishing/Echo-Essentials/tree/master/chapter1

Check out the following video to see the code in action:
https://goo.gl/QjupHX

HTTP basics

Two of the most critical structures within web application development are requests and responses. As with most other programs, a web application needs to take inputs, and produce outputs. As **HTTP** is a stateless protocol, each request made will result in a response message back to the caller. For a web application, the input comes in the form of an HTTP request, and the output as an HTTP response. The net/http package contains data structures that completely model the HTTP protocol message types, which are used by most of the many web frameworks built with Go. In the following diagram, you can see the HTTP request and response protocol data structures:

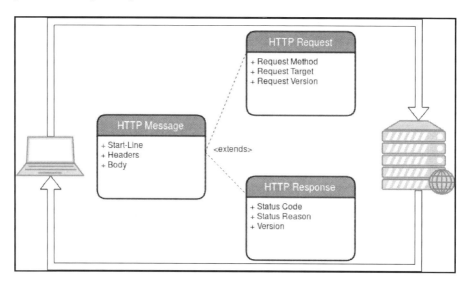

HTTP request

A request, as defined by *RFC-7230 Section 3*, is a text-based message, which includes the following required information at a minimum:

- **Request method (RFC-7231 4.3; RFC-5789 2)**: The method is the action the client would like to perform on the resource. Enumerated HTTP methods are a finite list of verbs, and are outlined in the preceding two RFCs. The Go `net/http` package contains a list of constants for referencing the various methods, as can be seen in the documentation: `https://golang.org/pkg/net/http/#pkg-constants`.

- **Request target (RFC-7230 5.3)**: The request target, derived from the **Uniform Resource Identifier** (**URI**), identifies the resource to which it applies the request on the server. This target, which is based on the specification, can consist of multiple parts, including a host portion, path portion, query portion, and fragment portion. The Go `net/url` package contains logic for parsing a **Unified Resource Locator** (**URL**), as can be seen in the documentation: `https://golang.org/pkg/net/url/`.

- **Request HTTP version (RFC-7230 2.6)**: The HTTP version is the textual representation of the highest minor version within the major version of the protocol that the client is able to support. Within the Go `net/http` web server, this version information is populated in the request type.

The following is an example of the plain text HTTP request message which will `GET` the resource `/file.txt` from the web server, from which the client would like to navigate to the `HTTP/1.1` protocol:

```
GET /file.txt HTTP/1.1
```

The first line in an HTTP message is known as the start-line of the HTTP message. If the message is a request type message, this line is more clearly known as the request-line of the message. As you can see in the Go documentation for the request type, the first five attributes of the `http.Request` type encompass the data from the start-line of the request: `https://golang.org/pkg/net/http/#Request`.

Additionally, and optionally, the request can contain the following data and metadata if applicable within the structure of the HTTP message:

- **Request header fields (RFC-7230 3.2)**: Request header fields, known as just headers, are key/value pairs of metadata associated with either of the HTTP message types, request or response. This metadata is used to further describe attributes of the request, such as the length of the content body, or authentication credentials. The key/value pairs are separated by a : character, and are enumerated directly after the start-line of the message, one line per pair. There is a helpful list of registered headers that are commonly in use, which can provide guidance on request and response metadata. These registered headers are defined here: http://www.iana.org/assignments/message-headers. Within the http.Request type, there is a Header attribute which is a key to value mapping.
- **Message body (RFC-7230 3.3)**: The message body is the payload of the request or response in the HTTP message protocol. The client and server are signaled the fact that the message body is present by the existence of the Content-Length or Transfer-Encoding headers. The Go web server implementation takes care of these headers automatically when a response is written to the response writer. The message body on a request is accessible from the Body attribute on the Request type in the net/http package. Of particular note here is that the Body is an implementation of the io.ReadCloser interface, which contains two methods: Read and Close.

The following is a more complete HTTP request message:

```
POST /file.txt HTTP/1.1
    Host: localhost
    Accept: */*
    Content-Length: 8
    Content-Type: application/x-www-form-urlencoded

    hi=there
```

In the preceding example, the request dictates that we want to use the POST method on the `/file.txt` target resource. Our request headers specify that we are attempting to contact a particular host which is localhost, and are willing to accept any type of response content. Since we have a request body that is URL encoded, we need a Content-Type header specifying the content type as well as the length of the request body in bytes. Finally, our request body, hi=there, is submitted as the message body of the HTTP request message.

HTTP response

Very similar to the request structure, responses also contain a start-line that is designated as the response status-line. The response may include a message body and header fields, just as the request message is capable of doing. The following data is included within the response line:

- **HTTP-Version (RFC-7230 2.6)**: Similar to the request HTTP-Version field in the request-line, the HTTP-Version is the protocol major and minor version in which the server is responding.

- **Status-Code (RFC-7231 6)**: The response status-code is a three-digit integer code that explains the response of the server. There are five different classes of status codes, namely informational (1xx), successful (2xx), redirection (3xx), client Error (4xx) and server error (5xx).

- **Reason-Phrase**: The reason-phrase of the response status-line should be ignored by the client, as it is a textual explanation concerning the status of the request.

Within Go, there is an `http.Response` type which contains all of the previously enumerated elements within the status-line as well as a response header structure and a message body. Typically, if you are developing a web application in Go, you will generally only interface with the response type through the `http.ResponseWriter` type defined (https://golang.org/pkg/net/http/#ResponseWriter), which is an interface. This interface allows the developer to populate the message header fields with the Header method, and write the status-line in the message with the `WriteHeader` method. If the response requires a message body in the response message, the `http.ResponseWriter` interface has a Write method which will send the raw data as the response message body.

When looking at web application frameworks, it is important to keep in mind the bare essentials of the protocol. The HTTP protocol is a very simple text-based protocol, consisting of request and response messages that were designed to be stateless. However, some very interesting and complex systems and services have been built on top of this simple protocol. When we talk about web frameworks and Echo, we need to keep in mind how the features will affect our application, which in the end is a simple text-based protocol.

Go HTTP handlers

At some point in your web application, when you are given a request, you will need to perform actions and provide a response to the request. Within the `net/http` package, there is an `http.Handler` interface which is implementable, allowing a common entry point scheme for the web server to run your handler code. The Go web server implementation effectively takes a handler you specify, and for each request it runs your handler's `ServeHTTP` method, which is defined in the interface. As seen in the documentation (https://golang.org/pkg/net/http/#Handler) the handler's `ServeHTTP` method signature includes a parameter for a `http.ResponseWriter` interface as well as a pointer to the `http.Request` structure. The following is an example handler implementation, which can be found at https://github.com/PacktPublishing/Echo-Essentials/tree/master/chapter1/SimpleHandler.go:

```
package main

import "net/http"

func main() {
 http.Handle("/", new(myHandler))
 http.ListenAndServe(":8080", nil)
}

type myHandler struct{}

func (mh *myHandler) ServeHTTP(w http.ResponseWriter, r *http.Request) {
 w.WriteHeader(200)
 w.Write([]byte("hello!"))
}
```

Within the preceding example, we are creating a handler type called `myHandler`, which implements the handler interface. In the implementation of `myHandler.ServeHTTP`, we are writing `hello!` as the response body back to the caller. To exercise this handler, you can run this code with `go run SimpleHandler.go` and then do the same in another terminal running `curl localhost:8080/`, which will make a request to this service.

Though simple, this example outlines a number of concerns for web application developers. One primary concern is wondering how you can use URL path variables such as `/resource/$ID`, where `$ID` would be a variable within your handler. What happens if your code panics within your handler? Are you responsible for encoding all of your response body payload into a `[]byte type`? How can you implement reusability if you need to run the same processes across multiple handlers?

Go HTTP web server

A web server's primary purpose is to accept HTTP request messages, process the requests, and respond with HTTP response messages. The web server that is built into the Go `net/http` package is a wonderful example of a bare bones web server. The web server listens for and accepts new TCP requests, launches a new Go routine for each request, and then runs the developer-specified handler for the request in the new Go routine. The web server implementation watches for any application-level panics that occur within the code and then sends the response generated by the handler code back to the client that initiated the request.

This works due to the lightweight thread scheduling that is done within the Go runtime environment. Go routines are much cheaper to initialize and run than traditional threads and subprocesses, and are designed so that thousands of Go routines can be running at the same time. The following is a high-level diagram of how a request is processed within the Go web server:

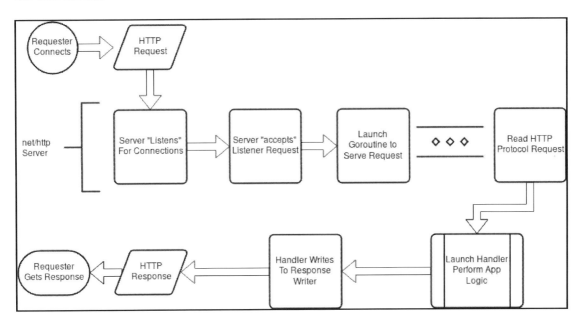

As a recap, the Go web server will spawn and execute each handler function within a Go routine for every single request that the web server receives. The Go web server will handle the network's listen and accept life cycles, and has a **Transport Layer Security** (**TLS**) built-in if requested by the developer.

Reasons for a framework

Due to the minimalist implementations within the net/http package, classic web application paradigms that developers have been employing for years in the industry are noticeably absent. This is not an oversight by the creators of the net/http package, but rather a feature. By keeping the functionality of the package stripped of higher level functionality, the developer building a web application has the flexibility to build solutions that fit their particular use cases.

This minimalism-based mindset does cause work for developers, in that higher level functionality must be built into the web application itself. An example would be middleware and request pipeline processing. This is common in many web application frameworks, and request pipelines have been implemented in a plethora of ways by various projects, all motivated by different priorities. Another example would be URL routing to handlers. Though an implementation exists in the standard library, it has been shown in the industry that the current embodiment within the net/http package is lacking in functionality for the majority of common use cases. Moreover, there are no helpers for common problems such as encoding and rendering responses, or binding request inputs to variables within a handler. Lastly, up until very recently, the net/http package did not have a mechanism by which request context could be kept throughout the request's lifetime.

Setting up the environment

In order to get started with Echo, you will need a working Go environment. To that end, installing Go in your environment is fairly trivial. Firstly, we need to download the Go source code and tool chain and install them. For this book, we will be using Go version 1.9.4, which is the latest release at the time of writing this book. As you can see at https://golang.org/doc/install, there are detailed instructions for setting up your environment correctly. The following are the typical steps needed to install Go for your system:

Linux/macOSX Go Installation

Download Go 1.9.4:

- Linux:

```
curl -O https://dl.google.com/go/go1.10.linux-amd64.tar.gz
sudo tar -C /usr/local -xzf go1.10.linux-amd64.tar.gz
```

- macOS using Homebrew:

    ```
    brew install go
    ```

Set up related environmental variables (assuming you use `bash`):

```
mkdir -p ~/go

echo "export GOPATH=$HOME/go" >> ~/.bashrc

echo "export PATH=$PATH:$HOME/go/bin:/usr/local/go/bin" >> ~/.bashrc

source ~/.bashrc
```

At this point, the environment is set up. The preceding `curl` command downloads Go as a tarball, and the `tar` command will unpack the Go standard library source code and related binary tools into the `/usr/local/go` directory on your system. If you are running this as a non-root user, you might need to run the tar command listed in the preceding snippet with root privileges, potentially by changing users to `root`, or running the command with `sudo`.

The preceding environment variable setup commands will first set up a workspace as a `go` directory within your home directory. The command will also set your `GOPATH` environment variable to use this workspace for downloading `go` packages. Next, we need to set the `PATH` variable to include the `bin` directory that was installed in `/usr/local/go/`, which is where the Go compiler, as well as other tools such as `gofmt` that come with Go, reside. Finally, we add all of these environment variables into your `.bashrc` so that every time you log in, these environment variables are set appropriately.

Windows installation

You can download the MSI installer for Go: `https://dl.google.com/go/go1.10.windows-amd64.msi`.

The Windows installer will, by default, install Go in the `c:\Go\` folder. The installer will take care of setting up all necessary environment variables for you.

Setting up Echo

After you have a working installation of Go, you will be able to install the Echo web application framework. To install third-party libraries and packages, you can use the `go get` command to get any package you need. The following is how you would go about installing Echo version 3.3.5, which is the latest version at the time of writing this book, and which is the version of Echo we will use for the remainder of this book:

```
go get github.com/labstack/echo

cd $GOPATH/src/github.com/labstack/echo

git checkout tags/3.3.5

cd -
```

The preceding commands will clone the Echo web application framework into your `GOPATH` in the appropriate location, and then checkout the 3.3.5 release tag of the repository. With the preceding command, we can ensure that we are using the correct version of Echo. Cloning the repository directly and checking out the appropriate version might seem a little bit annoying, but unfortunately the `go get` tool, at the time of writing, does not support versioned package downloads. In future chapter examples, we will utilize a version pinning tool that is extremely handy called `dep`, which will eliminate the need to perform these steps on a per project basis.

In order to verify that we have your environment completely set up, we will now create a small Echo-based web application, and compile it to prove we have a working setup. You can download the following code using `git` with the following commands:

```
mkdir -p $GOPATH/src/github.com/PacktPublishing/

cd $GOPATH/src/github.com/PacktPublishing/

git clone https://github.com/PacktPublishing/Echo-Essentials

cd Echo-Essentials
```

Now that you have the code, you will be able to see the following code located in the `./chapter1/environment_setup.go`: file:

```
package main
import (
 "net/http"
 "github.com/labstack/echo"
)
```

```go
func main() {
    // create a new echo instance
    e := echo.New()
    // Route / to handler function
    e.GET("/", handler)
    // start the server, and log if it fails
    e.Logger.Fatal(e.Start(":8080"))
}

// handler - Simple handler to make sure environment is setup
func handler(c echo.Context) error {
    // return the string "Hello World" as the response body
    // with an http.StatusOK (200) status
    return c.String(http.StatusOK, "Hello World")
}
```

Within this project, you may notice that all of the dependencies are already downloaded to the `./chapter1/vendor` directory. If you wanted to pull the dependencies yourself, this can be performed by running `go get ./...` from within the `$GOPATH/src/github.com/PacktPublishing/Echo-Essentials/chapter1/` directory. The `go get` command will walk through your source code recursively and pull all of the dependencies needed from the internet, based on the import statements from within your code. At this point, you should attempt to run the code with `go run environment_setup.go`, which should produce the following output:

```
go run $GOPATH/src/PacktPublishing/Echo-
Essentials/chapter1/environment_setup.go

   ____    __
  / __/___/ /  ___
 / _// __/ _ \/ _ \
/___/\__/_//_/\___/ v3.3.5
High performance, minimalist Go web framework
https://echo.labstack.com
                                  O/_____
                                  O\
⇒ http server started on [::]:8080
```

This output proves that we are properly configured for our Echo-based web application, and that we are using the correct version of Echo, that is Version 3.3.5.

Summary

At this point, we are ready to start diving into creating web applications using the Echo framework. Within this chapter, it has been shown how the base Go `net/http` standard library represents HTTP request and response types, web request handlers, as well as how the built-in Go web server works. Due to the minimalist implementation of Go's standard library, there exists the need for using a web application framework for handling common tasks, and increasing developer efficiencies. This chapter has also covered some basic environmental setup, as well as installation of a version-pinned Echo dependency.

The following chapters will go into depth about the features of the Echo framework, and include real-world examples of how Echo will allow you to create services efficiently and effectively that excel in performance and ease of development.

2
Developing Echo Projects

Of the most compelling reasons to use a web application framework for a project, the most important is that it offers clean, organized code. Frameworks offer defined structure for application development, as well as helpful functionality that minimizes the energy the developer has to use to create an application. Within an Echo project, the developer has the flexibility in implementation and project structure.

We will begin by diving into an example of an Echo project. Once we have the basic directory structure of our application defined, and the reasoning for the structure in place, we will begin to explore some fundamental building blocks and features of Echo in our example project. Firstly, we will cover target-path routing and application-handler development. Then, we will explain a high-level overview of the most commonly used features within Echo, including concepts of routing, middleware, bindings, and response rendering.

Within this chapter, the following concepts will be covered:

- Organizing an Echo project
- Defining and implementing Echo handlers
- High-level overview of the following features:
    - Routing
    - Middleware
    - Data binding and rendering

By the end of this chapter, you will have all of the knowledge necessary to start creating your own Echo project. You will have a working reference implementation of a non-trivial application that utilizes the key features within Echo in order to become immediately productive.

Developing Echo Projects

Technical requirements

You will be required to know Go programming language, also basics of web application framework. You will also need to install Git, in order use the Git repository of this book. And finally, ability to develop with an IDE on the command line.

The code files of this chapter can be found on GitHub:
`https://github.com/PacktPublishing/Echo-Essentials/tree/master/chapter2`

Check out the following video to see the code in action:
`https://goo.gl/NudCD9`

Setting up a project in echo and organizing code

The best way to learn is by example in my opinion, so, to that end, we will walk through the initial creation of an application to best showcase the Echo framework. The source code for our sample project for this chapter is located here: `https://github.com/PacktPublishing/Echo-Essentials/tree/master/chapter2`. The following is a preliminary use-case diagram showing the interactions we will be creating, which will help us develop this project:

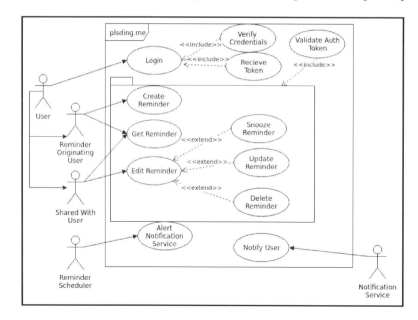

Regardless of the particulars of the project, organization of code is paramount for the success of the project. When we are developing a Go web application with Echo, it helps to start your project with a strong directory structure. A well-thought-out structure limits the number of issues with cyclical imports, and will allow you to create a clean in-project dependency tree. The organization must also be intuitive for collaboration with others. Web frameworks, such as Django for Python, have a very opinionated organization, which typically follows the Model–View–Controller paradigm. The need to separate business logic cleanly is also important, as well as persistence logic and the protocol-specific logic, including request and response structures.

If you have already downloaded the sample code repository from Chapter 1, *Understanding HTTP, Go, and Echo*, you can ignore the following commands, but if you have not, you can get the sample code by using `git` with the following commands:

```
mkdir -p $GOPATH/src/github.com/PacktPublishing

git clone https://github.com/PacktPublishing/Echo-Essentials
```

For our example application, we will structure our repository, as follows:

```
$GOPATH/src/github.com/PacktPublishing/Echo-Essentials/chapter2/
        bindings/
        cmd/
                service/
        handlers/
        middlewares/
        models/
        renderings/
        static/
```

The preceding structure is broken down intuitively, and allows for application growth. As you can see in the following internal dependency diagram, it shows a very clean import path for our previously defined packages. With the sample code downloaded, you can see that from within the chapter2/ directory in the repository that our code layout has the following structure:

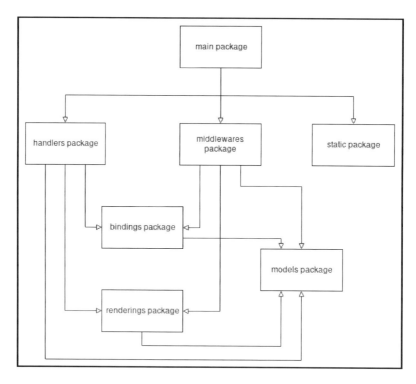

A brief commentary showing the reasoning for the structure is as follows:

- bindings

    - The bindings directory will hold all of the protocol-specific data bindings for the application, such as form submission, query string, and JSON representations of application input

    - It is fairly common to see generic application data models used for request and response types, but it is the opinion of the author that this causes issues when a developer wishes to version API definitions

- cmd
    - The cmd directory can be thought of as the "entrypoint" for the application. By separating the cmd/service package from the root package of the project, we are adding structure to allow for multiple applications in one project.
    - For example, if you wanted to implement the scheduler portion of the application as a standalone daemon that needs to use modules defined within the same repository, you are able to do so by creating a new cmd/scheduler package to handle this case.
    - Eventually, after a product is developed, it is often found that creating microservices is useful. With this cmd package, we would be able to easily create different packages which will become new executable services, and still use the existing codebase structure to support this task.
- handlers
    - The handlers package is where we will store all of our Echo web application-handler code and business logic for the application
- middlewares
    - The middlewares package is where we will store all of our Echo web application middleware code and business logic that is applicable for more than one handler within our service
    - Example middleware from our use-case diagram would be the "Verify Token" functionality, which will validate whether the requester is who they say they are.
- models
    - Within an application, you will have application-specific data structures that you will need to persist to a database for instance. The models package will house the application-specific types.

- The `models` package is separated from bindings and renderings, as you may wish to have both binding types and rendering types be based on a common model. This structure will make this easier.

- renderings

  - The `renderings` package will contain all of the data structures and types that will be serialized back to the caller through the `http.ResponseWriter`

- static

  - The `static` directory will contain all static assets and content that is required for the application. In some cases, you may want to render HTML templates to the caller. In other cases, you may need to serve JavaScript or images back to the caller. Within our Echo project, all of the static content we will reference will live in this "package".

Implementing a project

With the appropriate structure in place for our Echo project, we can get started by expanding on our simple example Echo application from Chapter 1, *Understanding HTTP, Go, and Echo*.

The following code is located in the `$GOPATH/src/github.com/PacktPublishing/Echo-Essentials/chapter2/cmd/service/main.go` file:

```
package main

import (
        "github.com/PacktPublishing/Echo-Essentials/chapter2/handlers"
        "github.com/labstack/echo"
)

func main() {
        // create a new echo instance
        e := echo.New()
        // Route / to handler function
```

```
            e.GET("/health-check", handlers.HealthCheck)
            // Authentication routes
            e.POST("/login", handlers.Login)
            e.POST("/logout", handlers.Logout)
            // start the server, and log if it fails
            e.Logger.Fatal(e.Start(":8080")) }
```

Within the preceding code block, a new Echo server is instantiated, and a route is added to the path /health-check, which will be routed to the handlers.HealthCheck function. Routing will be covered for our example application later on in this chapter, and then in much greater detail in Chapter 3, *Exploring Routing Capabilities*, later on in the book. Finally, the server is started on port 8080 on the final line of the main function. This code imports the handler module, which has a file called $GOPATH/src/github.com/PacktPublishing/Echo-Essentials/chapter2/handlers/health_check.go, as seen in the following code:

```
    package handlers

    import (
            "net/http"

            "github.com/PacktPublishing/Echo-Essentials/plsding.me/renderings"
            "github.com/labstack/echo"
    )

    // HealthCheck - Health Check Handler
    func HealthCheck(c echo.Context) error {
            resp := renderings.HealthCheckResponse{
                    Message: "Everything is good!",
            }
            return c.JSON(http.StatusOK, resp)
    }
```

The handlers package houses all of the API business logic in the form of Echo style handlers. As you may recall from Chapter 1, *Understanding HTTP, Go, and Echo*, Go's net/http package defines a handler function signature as a function that takes in an http.ResponseWriter and a *http.Request, which is very different than the handler shown in the preceding code. The handler type in Echo is a function that takes in an Echo Context, and returns an error. Within the Echo Context, we have access to the request, as well as the response writer if we wanted to access them directly. Echo also provides useful helpers methods off of the Echo Context. For example, c.JSON(in the preceding code takes the status parameter and an interface{}, and will render the provided interface{} as JSON before writing that result to the http.ResponseWriter for you!

You may also notice that we are importing the `renderings` package here. As mentioned previously, we designate all response structures to belong to this renderings package for ease of application development. Within the renderings directory is a file called `health_check.go`, which contains the following:

```
package renderings

type HealthCheckResponse struct {
        Message string `json:"message"`
}
```

This `HealthCheckResponse` structure contains one attribute called `Message`. It should be noted with this project layout structure that we can and should name all of our related files similarly to keep the code structure as intuitive as possible. Within the `handlers` directory, there is a `health_check.go` file, which will handle all of the health check-related application logic. Similarly, there is a renderings `health_check.go`, which will store all of the renderings related to the health check response structures.

Dependency management

One directory that we haven't mentioned so far is the `vendor` directory. The `vendor` directory in a Go project is a special directory. This is where dependency management for your project will be stored. For our book's long sample project, we will be using the `dep` tool. Concisely, `dep` is a dependency management tool that will allow you to version pin your dependencies to a project. It works by taking all of the imported packages that were retrieved with `go get` or git commands directly in your `$GOPATH` and copies the relevant source code needed by your project into this `vendor` directory within your project. The tool does this by reading your source code `import` statements and figuring out which packages you need. To get us started, we need to get the `dep` command with the following command:

```
go get -u github.com/golang/dep/cmd/dep
```

After we install the `dep` tool, we can initialize our project's `vendor` directory, as shown in the following code. When the `dep` tool initializes a project, it will take all of the dependencies you have imported and put the code in the `vendor` directory:

```
dep init
```

It is highly recommended that some form of dependency management is used within Go projects. There is nothing worse than a project build failure related to the removal of a dependency from the internet, such as the left-pad issue with NPM. You can avoid this type of issue by committing the `vendor` directory directly into your repository, and versioning it with the rest of your code. There are drawbacks to this approach—namely, that the size of pull and merge requests grow very large when there are significant changes to the dependencies of a project. It is the author's opinion, however, that these sorts of large dependency changes are indicative of possibly a larger workflow problem.

With this strong structural foundation in place, we are ready to begin the process of creating our application. The remainder of this chapter will briefly touch on the major features within the Echo framework.

Routing and handlers

When we think of routing, we often think of networking routers that send traffic on networks to their destinations. For the purposes of this book, when the term routing is used, the topic is how to map a target path to a handler function. There are many ways to do this, each with benefits and drawbacks. Sometimes, all you need is a static mapping of a target path string, such as `/reminder` to a function called `CreateReminder`. Then, any time a user visits your application with a target path of `/reminder`, your `CreateReminder` function will be triggered.

What happens, though, if you want to have a URL variable within the URL? For example, if we wanted to have `/reminder/123` relate to a reminder resource with an ID of `123`. It would be impractical to have all of the reminder IDs within the entire system mapped out by our target path router. You may consider performing a regular expression match within the target path router, `/reminder/\d+`, which will match `/reminder/123` and pass `123` in as a variable to the handler. This is a step in the right direction, but it is still lacking in that you will need to check every single target path in your application for every request until you find a match. Echo employs a different technique. Echo uses a Radix tree data structure to allow for more efficient searching based on the target path prefix. We will cover more about how in the chapter dedicated to routing.

Routing

For our project, we need to define `routes` to our handlers. We will continue our project by creating a login mechanism that will validate a user and return a token to our user if successful. The following is a code block from `$GOPATH/src/github.com/PacktPublishing/Echo-Essentials/chapter2/cmd/service/main.go`, which shows our new route:

```
e.GET("/health-check", handlers.HealthCheck)

    // Authentication routes
    e.POST("/login", handlers.Login)
    e.POST("/logout", handlers.Logout)
```

Within the Echo server instance, there are helper methods to add the target path to route to a handler. In our example, we are adding a login and logout entry to the Echo server's router. Whenever a HTTP POST request with a target path of `/login` comes into the server, the router will run the `handlers.Login` function.

Another important concept to touch on in routing is the concept of grouping. Within a project for an organization, you may consider lumping paths together by prefix. A prime example of doing this would be for path-based API versioning where you have a versioned string prefix of a path for a target path. In the following code snippet, we group the authentication routes in a `/v1/` prefix:

```
// Authentication routes
    g := e.Group("/v1")
    g.POST("/login", handlers.Login)
    g.POST("/logout", handlers.Logout)
```

Handlers

At this point, it is known that routes map target paths to handlers, but what are handlers? Handlers are the meat of web application development. A handler is primarily where the application converts input into output. As mentioned before, `net/http` defines a handler as an implementation of the `http.Handler` interface, implementing the `ServeHTTP` method with the following signature:

```
func (f Handler) ServeHTTP(w ResponseWriter, r *Request)
```

Echo has detoured from this model by creating its own interface for an `echo.HandlerFunc`, defined by the following signature:

```
type HandlerFunc func(Context) error
```

Following our example code, the following is an initial attempt at creating a handler for the `/login` resource of our application. This code is located in `handlers/login.go`:

```go
// Login - Login Handler will take a username and password from the request
// hash the password, verify it matches in the database and respond with a
token
func Login(c echo.Context) error {
        resp := renderings.LoginResponse{}
        lr := new(bindings.LoginRequest)

        if err := c.Bind(lr); err != nil {
                resp.Success = false
                resp.Message = "Unable to bind request for login"
                return c.JSON(http.StatusBadRequest, resp)
        }

        if err := lr.Validate(c); err != nil {
                resp.Success = false
                resp.Message = err.Error()
                return c.JSON(http.StatusBadRequest, resp)
        }
```

In our example handler function, we begin by setting up a response-rendering structure and a request binding. After we have created our binding structure, we use Echo's built-in `Bind` function call, which will take the request body payload and deserialize the payload into the structure passed into `Bind` as a parameter. After we convert the request payload into a data structure in the handler, we perform some validation on the request-binding data structure. In our case, our data structure has been designed to include a `Validate` function, as shown in the preceding code.

Now that we have a valid request data structure in our handler code, we can use that request to perform the handler function, which in the case of a typical login handler would be to draw user data from a database and perform hashing on the presented password to authenticate a user:

```go
        // get DB from context
        db := c.Get(models.DBContextKey).(*sql.DB)
        // get user by username from models
        user, err := models.GetUserByUsername(db, lr.Username)
        if err != nil {
                resp.Success = false
```

```
                resp.Message = "Username or Password incorrect"
                return c.JSON(http.StatusUnauthorized, resp)
        }

        if err := bcrypt.CompareHashAndPassword(
                user.PasswordHash, []byte(lr.Password)); err != nil {
                resp.Success = false
                resp.Message = "Username or Password incorrect"
                return c.JSON(http.StatusUnauthorized, resp)
        }
```

Echo provides an easy mechanism for drawing variables from the built-in Context object. With `c.Get`, we pull the `sql` database structure pointer from the Echo Context. We then take that database pointer and use the helper function we created in `models` to perform a `sql` request to the database. When we get the result back, which is a `models.User` structure from the database, we then take the `bcrypt` hashed password from the database and the plain text password we got from our caller and perform a compare of the two hashed values. Based on the results of that hash comparison, if successful, we then create a JWT token for the user to present in all future requests:

```
        // need to make a token, successful login
        signingKey := c.Get(models.SigningContextKey).([]byte)

        // Create the Claims
        claims := &jwt.StandardClaims{
                ExpiresAt: time.Now().Add(time.Hour * 72).Unix(),
                Issuer:    "service",
        }

        token := jwt.NewWithClaims(jwt.SigningMethodHS256, claims)
        ss, err := token.SignedString(signingKey)
        if err != nil {
                resp.Success = false
                resp.Message = "Server Error"
                return c.JSON(http.StatusInternalServerError, resp)
        }

        resp.Token = ss

        return c.JSON(http.StatusOK, resp)
}
```

The preceding code starts the `handlers.Login` function by creating a new `renderings.LoginResponse` and a new `bindings.LoginRequest`, which we then bind our request data from the HTTP request to. Echo has a `c.Bind` function on the Echo Context type, which takes the input from the request and populates the `bindings.LoginRequest` we pass in. After we bind and validate our structures, we perform the business logic of getting the user from the database. We perform a `bcrypt` operation, and, upon success, we generate a new JWT token which will be the authentication token returned to the user.

Handlers are where the business logic happens, and routing is how handlers are run in our service. The essence of a web application or API is confined within these two basic primitives.

Middleware

Sometimes, there are use cases where the same application logic needs to be applied to a multitude of resources within an application. A prime example of this type of logic is protecting resources behind an authentication mechanism. Some resources such as the login or static resources typically do not need this authentication logic, but other resources such as our reminder creation, snoozing, need to be protected by authentication. We can accomplish this feat with the use of middleware.

A middleware can be thought of as a wrapper for the handlers we create. An Echo middleware is defined as a function that takes the next function to call as a parameter, and returns an Echo handler. By having the parameter be the next handler function to call, we are able to build a chain of handlers:

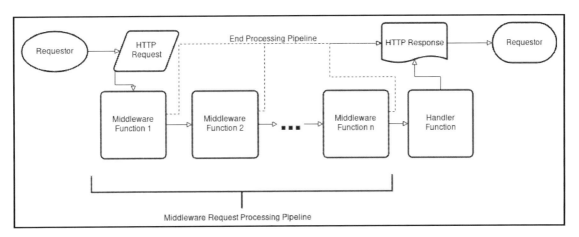

Custom middleware

Echo comes with a very rich set of contributed middleware functions that perform a wide variety of different tasks. Since we decided to use JWT tokens for our authentication mechanism defined in the prior section, we can take advantage of the JWT middleware that ships with Echo to force only valid, authenticated users the ability to call particular resources. The following shows a general middleware that sets the `signingKey` for our JWT on the context, so that our login handler has access to it. It also shows how we can use grouping to limit middleware functions to specific subsets of resources from within `$GOPATH/src/github.com/PacktPublishing/Echo-Essentials/chapter2/cmd/service/main.go`:

```go
// Signing Key for our auth middleware
var signingKey = []byte("superdupersecret!")
e.Use(func(next echo.HandlerFunc) echo.HandlerFunc {
    return func(c echo.Context) error {
        c.Set(models.SigningContextKey, signingKey)
        return next(c)
    }
})

reminderGroup := e.Group("/reminder")
reminderGroup.Use(middleware.JWT(signingKey))
reminderGroup.POST("", handlers.CreateReminder)
```

Middleware functions are a great way to enrich requests with common functionality that can be reused across application handler code. The use of middleware will significantly simplify your code and allow for greater reuse across your application.

Rendering

As mentioned previously, the job of a web application or an API is to create an HTTP response message, given an HTTP request message. Echo has a really nice facility to help us render responses from our handlers and middleware functions. `echo.Context` has methods which perform all of the heavy hitting for rendering responses back to the caller. As seen in prior examples, there is a `JSON` method on the Echo Context which allows for rendering of a JSON payload back to the caller. The following is a list of supported rendering capabilities within Echo:

- **HTML**: Render an HTML response:
    - **HTMLBlob**: Render a preformed HTML response

- **JSON**: Render a JSON response, converting the variable into JSON based on the `struct` tags of the variable:

    - **JSONBlob**: Render a preformed JSON response

    - **JSONPretty**: Render a pretty JSON response

    - **JSONP**: Render a JSONP response based on the `struct` tags of the variable

- **XML**: Render an XML response based on the `struct` tags of the variable:

    - **XMLBlob**: Render a preformed XML string

    - **XMLPretty**: Render a pretty XML document

- **File**: Render a file response:

- **Attachment**: Render an attachment response

- **Blob**: Render a byte blob as the response

- **String**: Render a string as the response

- **NoContent**: Do not render a response body

- **Redirect**: Render a redirect response pointing the result to another location

All of the preceding methods provided in Echo allow you flexibility in rendering your application. Within a typical API, you will likely use a structured response rendering mechanism such as JSON or XML. If you are working on a server-side rendered web application, the HTML response mechanisms with built-in template rendering may make more sense for your use case.

Summary

Within this whirlwind chapter, much was covered about setting up an Echo project, as well as fundamentals of developing within the Echo framework. Some primary features of the framework were discussed, and examples were used to expose the reader to the concepts.

It is clear, based on the examples that were used within this chapter, that the most important aspect for a successful web application is the code's layout and organization. We are able to focus more on the particular application logic associated with our application by using the Echo framework. There is less need to find solutions to already solved problems such as request middleware pipelines, routing of URL paths to application handlers, and taking input and rendering output effectively.

In the remainder of the book, we will be looking at the features of the Echo framework in greater depth. In the next chapter, we will start looking closely at the routing capabilities, and the best practices in the resource identifier for application-handler mapping.

3
Exploring Routing Capabilities

In a web application, routing is the process of mapping the path component of a **Uniform Resource Identifier** (**URI**) to the handler code that represents a given resource. There are many ways to implement this functionality, all with positive and negative consequences for performance, usability, and functionality. The Echo framework provides an efficient solution to this problem through the implementation of a Radix Tree. Other frameworks range in routing implementation by using regular expressions, maps, and other mechanisms to perform this mapping functionality.

Within this chapter, we will go through examples of how the routing capabilities within the Echo framework perform better than many other web application frameworks. We will dive into route organization, grouping of routes, and real examples of best practices when coming up with your routing. By the end of this chapter, you should have confidence with the following:

- How routing works within a web application:
    - How to effectively group routes within your web application
    - How to organize your application routes
- Internals and capabilities of the Echo router
- Comparisons with other routers:
    - Performance considerations
    - Functional considerations

Technical requirements

You will be required to know Go programming language, also basics of web application framework. You will also need to install Git, in order use the Git repository of this book. And finally, ability to develop with an IDE on the command line.

The code files of this chapter can be found on GitHub: `https://github.com/PacktPublishing/Echo-Essentials/tree/master/chapter3`

Check out the following video to see the code in action: `https://goo.gl/SPqBes`

Basic handler routing

As you may recall, a URI path component determines the resource representation for a web application. Within the HTTP request message structure, not only do we have a target in the request line, but we also have the requested method as well. HTTP methods, or verbs, explain the intent of the request to act on the resource identified by the target. Within the realm of application development, the `request` method, in conjunction with the target resource identifier, will determine what application code the service is supposed to run. To this end, we will start by talking about how to add route mappings to your Echo project, and more importantly, how Echo uses the information in the request to run your handlers.

Adding routes

The Echo instance's `Add` method allows the user to insert a new route into the router. The parameters include two string arguments, method and path, as well as an `echo.HandlerFunc` variable for which the resulting request routing match should map. Finally, a list of applicable middleware functions to apply to the processing pipeline is the last parameter. The `Add` method declaration can be seen as follows:

```
func (e *Echo) Add(method, path string, handler HandlerFunc, middleware
...MiddlewareFunc) *Route {
```

Though there is no input validation for the method parameter within Echo *RFC 7231, Section 4.3* defines allowable request methods that are acceptable. Moreover, the handler will not be mapped unless the HTTP method is one of the allowable methods within the aforementioned RFC. Go's `net/http` supplies a set of constants that can be used as parameters:

```
const (
        MethodGet     = "GET"
        MethodHead    = "HEAD"
        MethodPost    = "POST"
        MethodPut     = "PUT"
        MethodPatch   = "PATCH" // RFC 5789
        MethodDelete  = "DELETE"
        MethodConnect = "CONNECT"
        MethodOptions = "OPTIONS"
        MethodTrace   = "TRACE"
)
```

With this `Add` functionality, we are able to insert our application routes into the framework's router data structure. Though this can be comprehensive, Echo does expose a few helper methods for adding routes based on HTTP request methods. For each HTTP request method, there is a corresponding router method that wraps the `Add` function, which will provide a simple mechanism to map a particular method and resource target. The following are the request method helper functions that the Echo framework exposes for use:

```
func (e *Echo) CONNECT(path string, h HandlerFunc, m ...MiddlewareFunc) *Route
func (e *Echo) DELETE(path string, h HandlerFunc, m ...MiddlewareFunc) *Route
func (e *Echo) GET(path string, h HandlerFunc, m ...MiddlewareFunc) *Route
func (e *Echo) HEAD(path string, h HandlerFunc, m ...MiddlewareFunc) *Route
func (e *Echo) OPTIONS(path string, h HandlerFunc, m ...MiddlewareFunc) *Route
func (e *Echo) PATCH(path string, h HandlerFunc, m ...MiddlewareFunc) *Route
func (e *Echo) POST(path string, h HandlerFunc, m ...MiddlewareFunc) *Route
func (e *Echo) PUT(path string, h HandlerFunc, m ...MiddlewareFunc) *Route
func (e *Echo) TRACE(path string, h HandlerFunc, m ...MiddlewareFunc) *Route
```

As you can see, for every single HTTP request method that is outlined within *RFC 7231 Section 4.3*, there is a corresponding helper method on the Echo instance. There is also a special helper method, Any, which allows for a handler function and middleware chain to be applied to all request methods for a given path or target resource location:

```
func (e *Echo) Any(path string, handler HandlerFunc, middleware
...MiddlewareFunc) []*Route
```

Any effectively informs the Echo router that no matter what the method within the request is given for the path target resource, run this handler and use this chain of middleware functions. The intent here is for the use cases where you, as the developer, wish to perform all of the HTTP request method handling yourself, as opposed to having different handler functions for each method. It is important to note that you should not use the Any mapping assignment with any of the other method-specific assignment functions. For example, if you do the following, the Any assignment will overwrite the POST as it comes after the POST call:

```
e.POST("/reminder", handlers.CreateReminder)
e.Any("/reminder", handlers.Reminder)
```

How Echo routing works

As mentioned previously, Echo employs a Radix Tree data structure and search algorithm to find the correct handler for a given resource identifier. A Radix Tree is a prefix tree, where each parent node in the tree represents a prefix of the child node. In our use case, since we are obviously performing string matching, a prefix tree is the appropriate tool for the job. The following is an extremely simplified diagram that explains how a Radix Tree works for our book-long project:

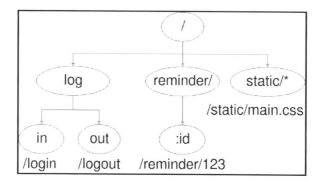

The preceding diagram assumes the following routes were added to our project, which can be seen in our sample code located
at: `$GOPATH/src/github.com/PacktPublishing/Echo-Essentials/chapter3/cmd/service/main.go`:

```
        // in order to serve static assets
        e.Static("/static", "static")

        // reminder handler group
        reminderGroup := e.Group("/reminder")
        reminderGroup.Use(middleware.JWT(signingKey))
        reminderGroup.POST("", handlers.CreateReminder)

        // Route / to handler function
        e.GET("/health-check", handlers.HealthCheck)
        // Authentication routes
        e.POST("/login", handlers.Login)
        e.POST("/logout", handlers.Logout)
```

As you can see, our root node is the / string, because all of our paths have / as a prefix, as all of the routes start with /. Next, we have a non-handler node with the prefix `log` that has two children, `in` and `out`. If you apply all of the prefixes to the leaf node `out`, you end up with the path `/logout`, which contains a reference to the `handlers.Logout` handler function. As you can see, the total depth of our tree is only three levels. This simple example doesn't do justice to the power of this data structure in this context, but if you have an extremely large API, such as the full GitHub API partially shown in the following snippet for brevity, you can understand how a prefix tree works for target routing:

```
└── /
    ├── r
    │   ├── epos
    │   │   ├── /
    │   │   │   └── :
    │   │   │       └── /
    │   │   │           └── :
    │   │   │               └── /
    │   │   │                   ├── events
    │   │   │                   ├── notifications
    │   │   │                   ├── s
    │   │   │                   │   ├── ta
    │   │   │                   │   │   ├── rgazers
    │   │   │                   │   │   └── t
    │   │   │                   │   │       └── s/
```

You may be asking, where does the HTTP request method come into play for selecting the appropriate handler within Echo? As we mentioned earlier, we very clearly articulate the method in the `Add` method, as well as in the helper named method functions. For historical context as well as to show how the framework has grown, when Echo was much younger, Echo actually kept a Radix Tree per HTTP method. This means that there was a separate data structure for GET routes, POST routes, as well as the other HTTP request methods. Echo would take the HTTP request method and isolate the appropriate tree to search for the endpoints based on said request method.

Unfortunately, this behavior led to an issue with RFC compliance, as stated in this pull request: `https://github.com/labstack/echo/pull/205`. The problem is that Echo would send a 404 Not Found response code to the requester in the event that said requester attempted to request a resource with an HTTP method that the API did not support. For example, say your API has a resource called `/reminder/123` and you did not want a user to be able to use the `POST` method to that resource. By using a separate Radix Tree per method, we would end up searching in the `POST` method Radix Tree only to find there is not a node with that prefix. Echo would then think that this resource doesn't exist and send back a 404 Not Found response. The correct behavior is to send back a 405 Method Not Allowed response code, as the resource does indeed exist; it just doesn't allow the `POST` HTTP request method.

Ultimately, Echo was changed for the better by altering the node data structure to include a `methodHandler` structure, which contained the per method handler mappings within each node of the tree. With this in place, Echo can maintain a single Radix Tree data structure for all methods. When a node is found, Echo can either respond back to the user that the method is not allowed if there is no handler associated with that particular request method, or perform the handler function associated with that resource and method.

Group routing

Alluded to earlier, there exists a grouping capability for defined routes within the Echo framework. Grouping of routes allows for simple logical groupings of sets of resources with a base prefix. A great example that works well with grouped routes is when you wish to have a target resource path versioned API, such as providing `/v1/login` and `/v1/logout`, as well as `/v2/login` and `/v2/logout`. This happens to be a very common way in which developers can prevent breakage of their API from major changes to the API. Typically, if the schema of the request or response changes, it is a best practice to create a new version of those resource targets. This helps identify to developers integrating with your API that there is a breaking change between the two APIs.

In this example, we would create a /v1/ and a /v2 group with the Group method, which is declared in the following code within Echo:

```
func (e *Echo) Group(prefix string, m ...MiddlewareFunc) (g *Group) {
```

Within this Group method call, we must provide a prefix string as well as an optional middleware chain that is applicable to this group of resources. The Group return value contains a number of methods; most importantly are exactly the same route mapping functions that we are given with Echo: Add, Any, GET, POST, PUT, and so on. The following is a more fleshed out example based on our example project, which can be seen in the $GOPATH/src/github.com/PacktPublishing/Echo-Essentials/chapter3/cmd/service/main.go file:

```
// V1 Routes
v1 := e.Group("/v1")
// V1 Authentication routes
v1.POST("/login", handlers.Login)
v1.POST("/logout", handlers.Logout)
// V1 Reminder Routes
v1Reminders := v1.Group("/reminder", middleware.JWT(signingKey))
v1Reminders.POST("", handlers.CreateReminder)
```

As you can see, grouping allows flexibility in defining responsible API resource target paths. First off, we create our main Echo instance group with the prefix of /v1, upon which we are adding /login and /logout. A very handy feature within the framework is the ability to create groups within groups. You can see that our /reminder is created off of our /v1 group.

Under the covers, the grouping mechanism merely wraps the Echo instance's Add function. This means that all group routes are applied to the Echo router's tree data structure by first applying the prefix of the group onto the path, and then inserting the routes into the Echo instance's router.

Regardless of whether you choose grouped routes or enumerating each route in full, understand that your routes will be matched identically. It is fairly common for API endpoints to allow either a trailing slash, or to not depend on the caller's personal preference. Based on our discussion so far, it is easy to see how this could cause problems, as our router will perform exact string matching based on the provided path. If, for example, we have a route set up, shown as follows, and we perform an HTTP call with a trailing slash, we will run into a Not Found situation:

```
e.POST("/login", handlers.Login)
```

Exploring Routing Capabilities

If we perform a call to this service, as shown in the following code, you will get a Not Found HTTP response code in the response. This is due to the fact that we do not have an exact match to /login in our request target path:

```
curl -XPOST http://localhost:8080/login/ -D -
HTTP/1.1 404 Not Found
Content-Type: application/json; charset=UTF-8
Date: Sun, 06 May 2018 16:22:09 GMT
Content-Length: 23

{"message":"Not Found"}
```

It is fairly typical for APIs to accept both versions, a trailing slash as well as a no trailing slash, and route them to the same handler. This, however, would become cumbersome if we created two routes for every single endpoint we wished to serve from the service. A good solution for this is to use the TrailingSlash middleware that comes bundled with Echo. We will explain how to use this middleware in depth within Chapter 4, *Implementing Middleware*, but using a middleware solution like TrailingSlash will allow you to outline your routes either with a trailing slash, or not, and the middleware will take care of the trailing slash for you prior to routing.

Considerations such as these must be in your mind when creating new APIs for consumption. To that end, the next section of this chapter will outline in detail particular implementation considerations for target path routers and attempt to shed some light on the positives and negatives related to different implementations.

Router implementation considerations

If you perform a search for Go Frameworks, you will come across a variety of different solutions, all with slightly different routing implementations. Luckily, based on https://github.com/julienschmidt/go-http-routing-benchmark, we have a mechanism by which we can pit all of these routers against each other to see which performs the best and which performs the worst under certain situations. Using these benchmarks when I was initially investigating router capabilities, the benchmarks provided gave some excellent insight into the efficiencies of the various routers from 2015:

```
BenchmarkAce_GithubAll 93675 ns/op 167 allocs/op
BenchmarkBear_GithubAll 264194 ns/op 943 allocs/op
BenchmarkBeego_GithubAll 1109160 ns/op 2092 allocs/op
BenchmarkBone_GithubAll 2063973 ns/op 8119 allocs/op
BenchmarkDenco_GithubAll 83114 ns/op 167 allocs/op
BenchmarkEcho_GithubAll 38662 ns/op 0 allocs/op
```

```
BenchmarkGin_GithubAll         43467 ns/op    0 allocs/op
BenchmarkGocraftWeb_GithubAll  386829 ns/op   1889 allocs/op
BenchmarkGoji_GithubAll        561131 ns/op   334 allocs/op
BenchmarkGoJsonRest_GithubAll  490789 ns/op   2940 allocs/op
BenchmarkGoRestful_GithubAll   15569513 ns/op 7725 allocs/op
BenchmarkGorillaMux_GithubAll  7431130 ns/op  1791 allocs/op
BenchmarkHttpRouter_GithubAll  51192 ns/op    167 allocs/op
BenchmarkHttpTreeMux_GithubAll 138164 ns/op   334 allocs/op
BenchmarkKocha_GithubAll       139625 ns/op   843 allocs/op
BenchmarkMacaron_GithubAll     709932 ns/op   2315 allocs/op
BenchmarkMartini_GithubAll     10261331 ns/op 2686 allocs/op
BenchmarkPat_GithubAll         3989686 ns/op  32222 allocs/op
BenchmarkPossum_GithubAll      259165 ns/op   812 allocs/op
BenchmarkR2router_GithubAll    240345 ns/op   1182 allocs/op
BenchmarkRevel_GithubAll       1203336 ns/op  5918 allocs/op
BenchmarkRivet_GithubAll       247213 ns/op   1079 allocs/op
BenchmarkTango_GithubAll       379960 ns/op   2470 allocs/op
BenchmarkTigerTonic_GithubAll  931401 ns/op   6052 allocs/op
BenchmarkTraffic_GithubAll     7292170 ns/op  22390 allocs/op
BenchmarkVulcan_GithubAll      271682 ns/op   609 allocs/op
BenchmarkZeus_GithubAll        748827 ns/op   2648 allocs/op
```

It is pretty clear that in my initial testing of the various web application frameworks, the Gin and Echo frameworks were the best performers with large API definitions. Echo was able to resolve a route within its router implementation within 38,662 nanoseconds on average, which is incredibly fast. Moreover, Echo is able to offer a zero allocations per call abstraction. In order to achieve zero allocations per call, Echo reuses context in a context pool. We will discuss that in Chapter 4, *Utilizing the Request Context and Data Bindings*.

Interestingly, one of the most popular routers is the Gorilla Mux router from the Gorilla web toolkit, which is a collection of independent tools which can be used to create web applications. Gorilla Mux, as seen in the preceding code, performs fairly poorly compared to some of the other high-performance routers, taking an average of 7,431,130 nanoseconds to resolve a route, which is 175 times slower than Echo's router implementation for the full GitHub API. This slowness has everything to do with the implementation of the router. Gorilla Mux uses a regular expression-based routing engine, much like the Django web framework in Python. For every request that comes in, Gorilla Mux will iterate over all of the regular expressions it holds for routes, and check to see if the request matches.

Though seven milliseconds does not seem like much to be worried about from a speed perspective, you have to realize that this is seven milliseconds of computation per request. If you have many requests, you will waste more and more time just trying to isolate which handler to run for the request. Since routing is performed on every single request, we need to keep an eye on performance.

You should always use the best tool for the job when writing a web application, and there are many times when a Radix Tree does not make sense for API endpoint routing. Since a search from a Tree takes `O(k)`, where `k` is the length of the string being searched within the tree, exceedingly long endpoint paths might have negative performance issues compared to a Hash Map data structure, which is built into the standard library.

In action

When implementing routing for your API or web application within the Echo Framework, it is important to keep routes logically separated with grouping, used for functional differences in the application, and/or versioning purposes. It is important to remember how the router implements the mapping, and in Echo's case since Echo uses a Radix Tree, the more similar prefixes you use within your API definition, the better the routing performance will be for your application. This is important to note in your API URL design because it will have important performance ramifications.

One item that has been left out of our routing discussion so far is how Echo handles URL parameters. You use a URL parameter when you need to have a variable length argument for your API located within the target path itself. This is very useful in API design, as you may want to reference a resource by an identifier in the URL path itself. In the following code, we will show you how to use the Echo router to pass this URL parameter to the handler. This example comes from the `$GOPATH/src/github.com/PacktPublishing/Echo-Essentials/chapter3/cmd/service/main.go` file:

```
v1Reminders.GET("/:id", handlers.GetReminder)
// /v1/reminder/:id
```

As seen in the preceding code, we are able to add a variable to the URL by using the `:` and then an identifier. In our example, we have our `/v1` and nested `/reminder` group, and a `GET` handler mapped to `/:id`. With this in place, the router will route any request GET method with the target path set to `/v1/reminder/:id` to the `handlers.GetReminder` handler function. To access this variable within the handler, we can use the `Context.Param` method to access the path parameter by name, as seen in the following `GetReminder` handler:

```
func GetReminder(ctx echo.Context) error {
        ctx.Logger().Info("Reminder id is: ", ctx.Param("id"))
        return nil
}
```

An interesting idea for the versioning of API routes would be to use a parameter for the version number of the API. By making the version number a URL parameter, you would no longer need to enumerate every single version within the main entry point of your application. This will give you flexibility, as well as improve the routing performance in your application. For example, you could do the following:

```
e.GET("/v:version/reminder/:id", GetReminder)
func GetReminder(c echo.Context) error {
        switch c.Param("version") {
               case "1":
                       return GetReminderV1(c)
               case "2":
                       return GetReminderV2(c)
}
```

In addition to parameter variables, there are also wildcard capabilities within the Echo router. Wildcard routes will match all requests so long as the prefix of the request URL matches. An example of using a wildcard would be `e.GET("/something/*" ...`, which would match any `GET` request that has a target that is prefixed by `/something/`. The `*` character represents a wildcard. Typically, the best use cases for wildcards are for serving static pages, as can be seen with our use of the `Static` Echo method earlier for serving our static content.

Implemented within Echo, the parameter and wildcard capabilities are handled somewhat differently than normal prefix strings. Within the routing implementation, the router takes on the insert name of the parameter you pass to the router using the `Add` or other helper methods, and stores the parameter name within the node as metadata on insert. For example, `e.GET("/reminders/:id", handlers.GetReminder)` is broken down into the search string `/reminders/:`, and the `id` is stored in the node's metadata in an indexed list of parameter names.

When a request comes in that matches the /reminders/ prefix and has input after the slash, the remainder of that path is stored in an indexed list as the parameter value. Within this implementation, when you perform a `Param` call in your handler, Echo takes the string value of the parameter name you are attempting to access, figures out which index that parameter name is located in, and returns the parameter value which resides at the same index in the parameter values list. This index parameter name/value pair of lists makes creating routes that contain several entries very simple. As a concrete example, the following is a route, and directly following that is a representation of the node within the Echo router:

```
e.GET("/i/:verb/with/a/:adjective/:noun", ParameterMadlibHandler)

func ParameterMadlibHandler(c echo.Context) error {
    return c.String(http.StatusOK,
        fmt.Sprintf("I %s with a %s %s!",
            c.Param("verb"),
            c.Param("adjective"),
            c.Param("noun"),
        ),
    )
}
```

The corresponding node after insertion would contain a list of parameter names that would look like the following:

```
["verb", "adjective", "noun"]
```

Now, when a request comes into the service that matches /i/:/with/a/:/:, the router will maintain a list of parameter values and map each : value to the corresponding named parameter. The following is an example HTTP call that exercises this route:

```
curl http://localhost:8080/i/run/with/a/tall/woman -D -
HTTP/1.1 200 OK
Content-Type: text/plain; charset=UTF-8
Date: Sun, 06 May 2018 17:02:31 GMT
Content-Length: 24

I run with a tall woman!
```

Wildcards are handled in a similar fashion, except there is no concept of a named wildcard. Because of this, wildcards are best used to match any suffix. It is not practical to do the following because you will not have easy access to the values:

```
e.GET("/i/*/from/a/*/*", WildcardMadlibHandler)
```

Though the preceding code will work, you will lose the ability to easily reference the values you are Glob matching within the handler. This is why typically you would use a * to reference a variable suffix on a route.

Summary

Resource target routing is a complicated problem that can be solved in many different ways. When creating a web application with Echo, you can rest assured that the routing will allow you the flexibility you need to nest your logical groupings of routes. You can also take solace in the fact that the overhead related to the routing of your API will be very low, both in performance and allocations per request.

Within the next chapter, we will discover the benefits of having a built-in middleware chaining solution within the Echo framework. We will also take a look at all of the excellent contributed middleware functions that are included with the web framework that will help with logging, error handling, and authentication and authorization mechanisms.

4
Implementing Middleware

Middleware is an important concept in web application development, and when implemented properly, this can result in efficient code reuse. By implementing and employing middleware within your application, you will benefit from an overall reduction in the complexity of your handler code, as well as duplication. This is achieved by taking discrete units of work that are useful to multiple handlers and putting that functionality into middleware that wrap your handlers.

Within this chapter, we will explore common request and response processing pipelines within web applications utilizing Echo's middleware framework. You will be given examples of how Echo middleware chaining works, as well as how implementing middleware will make your application simpler and more maintainable. You will also learn more about available middleware implementations that come with Echo that are immediately useful within your application.

After reading this chapter, you will have the confidence to perform the following skills within your web application:

- Create middleware and effectively implement business logic within it
- Understand Echo's middleware pipeline
- Organize Echo middleware to simplify application handlers
- Use contributed middleware from Echo

Technical requirements

You will be required to know Go programming language, also basics of web application framework. You will also need to install Git, inorder use the Git repository of this book. And finally, ability to develop with an IDE on the command line.

The code files of this chapter can be found on GitHub: `https://github.com/PacktPublishing/Echo-Essentials/tree/master/chapter4`

Check out the following video to see the code in action: `https://goo.gl/u5TBL3`

Basics of middleware processing

Within a web application, a request message is ingested and a response is produced, as has been reinforced in prior chapters. Typically, within handlers, there are fairly common tasks associated with the ingest of a request. Common request tasks include request body parsing and data binding, logging of requests, validating request authentication and session management, and request metadata creation. Conversely, common response-related tasks include request body rendering, as well as graceful error and panic handling. When you start looking at the common overhead associated with handling a request and generating a response, you can start seeing potential reuse cases.

As a concrete example, we have two handlers, `CreateReminder` and `GetReminder`, which parse requests, validate that the user's session is authentic and valid, perform request pedigree logging, and then perform the particular business logic for the given handler before rendering a response. In our particular example, one might try to solve the duplication of code by creating helper functions to perform the various overhead functionality. Though this is a fine solution, we are still left with much duplication in each handler, and are calling the same helper functions within each handler. Though the code is reusable, the handler is still riddled with helper function calls. Moreover, when one of the helper function signatures changes, we must touch all of the handlers that use those helper functions to refactor, which is not optimal.

A much better solution is to take all of these common overhead functionalities completely out of the handler code and allow our handlers to be somewhat ignorant of the complexities involved. Echo does provide some of this overhead handling for us with the `Context.Bind` functionality, which we will discuss in the next chapter, which is all about handling the binding of request parameters. The handler does not need to know how or when the parsing of the request structure occurs, as the framework handles this functionality.

Luckily, Echo's middleware implementation allows us the ability to inject functions before and after a handler is run. As seen in the following diagram, this is how a request middleware pipeline would work:

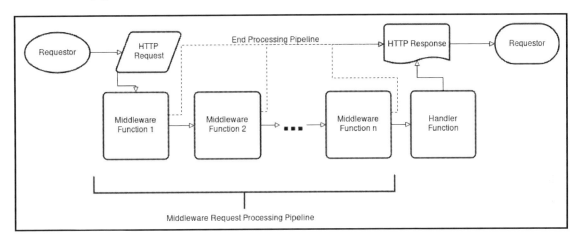

After Basics of Middleware Processing Image:

As a concrete example of how this helps reduce the amount of code for each handler, let's consider the following example of our two handlers so far, HealthCheck and Login, as though we want to add a RequestID for tracing purposes. The following are the beginning of the two handlers with the generation of a RequestID that we will reference in log messages:

handlers.HealthCheck:

```
    // HealthCheck - Health Check Handler
    func HealthCheck(c echo.Context) error {
            requestID := uuid.NewV4()
            c.Logger().Infof("RequestID: %s", requestID)

            resp := renderings.HealthCheckResponse{
                    Message: "Everything is good!",
            }
            return c.JSON(http.StatusOK, resp)
    }
```

handlers.Login:

```
    // Login - Login Handler will take a username and password from the request
    // hash the password, verify it matches in the database and respond with a
    token
```

Implementing Middleware

```
func Login(c echo.Context) error {
        requestID := uuid.NewV4()
        c.Logger().Infof("RequestID: %s", requestID)
//...
```

As you can see, within both handlers we are duplicating code, firstly to create a new UUID and secondly to log that UUID to our logging facilities. By using Echo middleware capabilities, we can consolidate this code within a middleware function, as shown in the following code:

```
const (
        RequestIDContextKey = "request_id_context_key"
)

func RequestIDMiddleware(next echo.HandlerFunc) echo.HandlerFunc {
        return echo.HandlerFunc(func(c echo.Context) error {
                requestID := uuid.NewV4()
                c.Logger().Infof("RequestID: %s", requestID)
                c.Set(RequestIDContextKey, requestID)
                return next(c)
        })
}
```

`RequestIDMiddleware` allows us to consolidate common functions across handlers, thereby reducing the amount of code needed to have the same functionality in multiple handlers. With the preceding middleware implementation, our handlers do not even need to know that this functionality is in place, and our handler code becomes much cleaner, as shown in the following code:

`handlers.HealthCheck`:

```
// HealthCheck - Health Check Handler
func HealthCheck(c echo.Context) error {
        resp := renderings.HealthCheckResponse{
                Message: "Everything is good!",
        }
        return c.JSON(http.StatusOK, resp)
}
```

By creating middleware, we can effectively intercept request processing before it reaches the handler function, and perform any business logic we want without the handler knowing about it. This is extremely useful for cases such as authentication and authorization, where we might wish to stop handling a request before it even reaches the handler if the caller is not authorized for the request. Within the next section, we will be talking about how middleware chaining works within the Echo framework in depth, as well as how we can insert middleware into our web application.

Middleware chaining

The Echo framework provides three mechanisms for inserting middleware into your request-processing pipeline. The Echo instance's `Use(MiddlewareFunc)` helper method is the most common way to add normal post-routing middleware. As you may recall, for flexibility we showed you how to use the `Group(string)` Echo method to organize routes. The `Use(MiddlewareFunc)` helper method is also available on Group instances so that you can apply middleware functions only to particular groupings of routes as well. `Use` tells the Echo instance, or grouping instance, that we wish to insert the middleware specified as a parameter into our middleware chain. It should be made clear that the order of your `Use` calls is very important. The order of the middleware insertion stipulates the order in which the middleware chain will be performed. For example, you might want two middleware, `Logger` and `Recover`, wrapping all of your routes. If you perform the following operations in order, and there is a `panic` within your `Logger` middleware, it will not be recoverable, as `Recover` is wrapped by `Logger`, and not vice versa. The following example can be found in $GOPATH/src/github.com/PacktPublishing/Echo-Essentials/chapter4/cmd/service/main.go:

```
e.Use(middleware.Logger())   // logger middleware will "wrap" recovery
e.Use(middleware.Recover()) // as it is enumerated before in the Use calls
```

Implementing Middleware

The Echo instance also provides `Pre(MiddlewareFunc)` too, which allows insertion of middleware functions prior to the routing step. This is for global, non-route-specific middleware functions. An example use case for this feature would be to manipulate the request prior to routing the request within the framework. As a concrete example, you would use this feature to change the URL or target path to remove trailing slashes or perform a redirect. Another good example of a reason to use Pre-Middleware is for things like recover handling from panics within your web application, so that responses do not comprise of stack traces. The `Pre` function works in the same way the `Use` function does, in that the ordering is important to how the middleware is chained. The earlier the `Pre` call, the earlier the middleware starts.

The third way to insert a middleware chain is by specifying particular middleware in order as variadic parameters on the handler routing insertion calls such as `GET`, `POST`, `Add`, and `Any`, as specified in the prior chapter. The ordering of the middleware specified in this variadic parameter is the order in which the processing will occur. It is important to note that this mechanism will only assign middleware to the specific route that is being inserted at the moment. Echo does this by composing the chaining of middleware by nesting the middleware function calls, as shown in the following code, which is also located within `$GOPATH/src/github.com/PacktPublishing/Echo-Essentials/chapter4/cmd/service/main.go`:

```
e.GET("/", HandlerFunction, Middleware1, Middleware2, Middleware3)
// RouteHandler = Middleware1(Middleware2(Middleware3(HandlerFunction)))
```

The following is an image that describes the call stack of the middleware chain we have built:

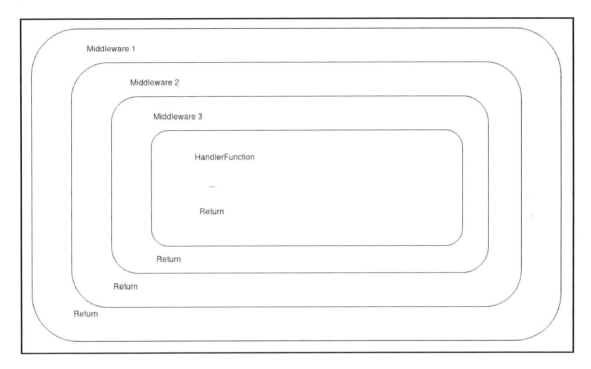

It is important to clarify that there are four logical boundaries where middleware can be applied from an API design standpoint:

- Global Middleware Before Routing
- Global Middleware After Routing
- Grouped Route Middleware
- Route Specific Middleware

Though there are four logical boundaries to think about when using middleware applications, within the Echo implementation, there are really only two. There's middleware that is run before routing, and middleware that is applied to a processing chain that ends in the handler running. Fortunately though, Echo allows us to use the four logical boundaries, as it manages the insertion of routes and handlers into our web application. It is during this insertion, at insertion time, where Echo applies the wrapping of middleware. So, internally you only ever have two places where middleware functions are applied, before routing or after routing.

Implementing Middleware

The following is an example of how Echo achieves middleware processing. You will notice that we start with a client request, which is accepted by the server. The server then kicks off the **Pre-Middleware** chain, which happens before routing occurs. Each middleware is run in order, and it is the responsibility of the middleware to call the `next` function, which is passed in as a parameter. Echo will build the function call chain and add the `next` middleware until there are no more in the list of middleware to be run. The **Pre-Middleware**, when completed, along with the chain then calls the router in order to find the handler. When the router finds the appropriate route within its search tree, the router then calls the handler function which has been wrapped by the middleware specified for that particular route. When it initiates the middleware chain associated with the particular route, it is possible at any point in the process where the middleware function is being run to return, thus causing the middleware chain to unwind backwards through the call stack until all of the middleware functions complete, resulting in a response to the caller:

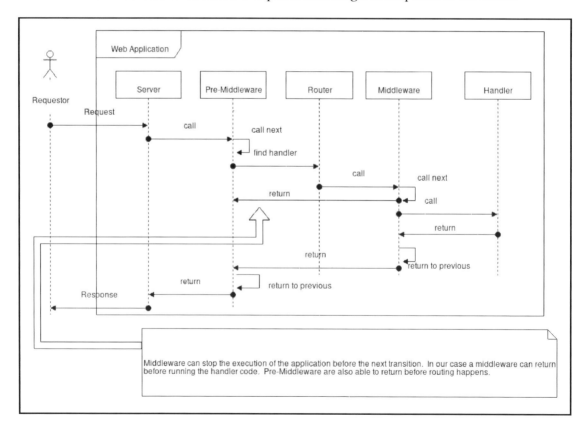

It is important to note that there is nothing magical about middleware within Echo. Middleware can be boiled down to an ordered set of nested function calls of which the handler is the last nested function call.

Creating custom middleware

Middleware functions are just functions that take in a `next` function and return a function. We are able to do this in Go because functions are first-class citizens, and they can be used as variables. By using this idea, we are able to use regular functions as parameters to middleware functions.

In order to create custom middleware for use within the Echo framework, all we need to do is create a function that conforms to the `echo.MiddlewareFunc` type, which is as follows:

```
type MiddlewareFunc func(HandlerFunc) HandlerFunc
```

The `echo.MiddlewareFunc` type which defines what a middleware should be is simply a function which takes a `next` parameter and returns a handler function. In the following example, we are creating a custom middleware which will assign a unique ID to every request that is made, and set our generated unique ID into the `echo.Context` for use in later stages of the request pipeline. The following code is found in the `$GOPATH/src/github.com/PacktPublishing/Echo-Essentials/chapter4/middlewares/request_id.go` directory within our project:

```
package middlewares

import (
        "github.com/labstack/echo"
        uuid "github.com/satori/go.uuid"
)

const (
        requestIDContextKey = "request_id_context_key"
)

func RequestIDMiddleware(next echo.HandlerFunc) echo.HandlerFunc {
    return echo.HandlerFunc(func(c echo.Context) error {
      requestID := uuid.NewV4()
      c.Logger().Infof("RequestID: %s", requestID)
      c.Set(RequestIDContextKey, requestID)
      return next(c)
    })
}
```

Implementing Middleware

A middleware that performs this functionality should be inserted early in the middleware call chain, in my opinion. I feel it needs to be inserted early because every single request that comes into the system should have a unique ID. For that reason, it makes sense that this middleware be a *Pre-Middleware*, which is processed before any routing occurs. In order to add this middleware as a Pre-Middleware so that every request before routing is performed gets a unique request ID, we add the following line to our `$GOPATH/src/github.com/PacktPublishing/Echo-Essentials/chapter4/cmd/service/main.go` **main entrypoint**:

```
e.Pre(middlewares.RequestIDMiddleware)
```

At this point, we are able to pull this newly generated unique request ID from the context inside any of our handlers. The power of `echo.Context` will be explored within Chapter 4, *Developing Echo Projects*, but for our sake, `echo.Context` is a place where state can be stored, and we can create the said state from within our middleware functions. The following is an example of how we can retrieve the `RequestID` that we created in the `middlewares.RequestIDMiddleware` from `handlers.HealthCheck`:

```
// HealthCheck - Health Check Handler
func HealthCheck(c echo.Context) error {
    if requestID, ok := c.Get(middlewares.RequestIDContextKey).(uuid.UUID); ok {
        c.Logger().Infof("RequestID: %s", requestID)
    }
    resp := renderings.HealthCheckResponse{
            Message: "Everything is good!",
    }
    return c.JSON(http.StatusOK, resp)
}
```

As you can see, when we query the `/health-check` endpoint, we get a new debug entry which shows the `RequestID` that was generated by our middleware, completely accessible from our handler:

```
{"time":"2018-03-15T23:52:55.19648893-04:00","level":"INFO","prefix":"echo","file":"echo.go","line":"478","message":"RequestID: bc9b2366-22bc-4480-a8e4-d325f1516003"}
```

Now that we have this simple custom middleware, we can start looking at some of the contributed middleware functions that come with the Echo framework. As mentioned previously, Echo comes with many useful middleware solutions that provide much functionality to make our web application development easier.

In action

Within the Echo project, there is a directory called `middleware`, which contains many contributed middleware solutions seen here: https://github.com/labstack/echo/tree/master/middleware. These middleware functions have been vetted by the community, and follow the middleware best practices guidelines. In this section, we will dissect one very useful middleware, and show how to use these middleware in our example application.

We will start by looking at `middleware.JWT`, which is a very helpful middleware that takes a **JSON Web Token (JWT)** from the request header specified by the developer and validates that the token is legitimate. In our example, the `handlers.Login` handler will validate the user credentials with bcrypt, and after that verification, we will create a JWT for the caller to insert into their request headers. The following is the JWT creation code located in `$GOPATH/src/github.com/PacktPublishing/Echo-Essentials/chapter4/handlers/login.go`:

```go
// need to make a token, successful login
signingKey := c.Get(models.SigningContextKey).([]byte)

// Create the Claims
claims := &jwt.StandardClaims{
        ExpiresAt: time.Now().Add(time.Hour * 72).Unix(),
        Issuer:    "service",
}

token := jwt.NewWithClaims(jwt.SigningMethodHS256, claims)
ss, err := token.SignedString(signingKey)
if err != nil {
        resp.Success = false
        resp.Message = "Server Error"
        return c.JSON(http.StatusInternalServerError, resp)
}

resp.Token = ss

return c.JSON(http.StatusOK, resp)
```

Implementing Middleware

After we have this JWT token created, on successful login, our client can attach this token to the `Authentication` request header with the `Bearer` authentication scheme for subsequent requests. Taking our example back to inserting the middleware, the following inside `$GOPATH/src/github.com/PacktPublishing/Echo-Essentials/chapter4/cmd/service/main.go` will allow us to insert the JWT middleware that comes with Echo in order to validate (for the specific group of routes denoted) that the request contains the correct authentication information:

```
// Latest Reminder Routes
reminderGroup := e.Group("/reminder")
reminderGroup.Use(middleware.JWT(signingKey))
```

As you can see, we are assigning our `/reminder` group, which includes all of the API endpoints for reminder manipulation and retrieval to use the Echo-contributed `middleware.JWT` middleware. This change has the effect that every single route that is within the reminder group will have the JWT authentication middleware applied, which performs this code to validate the JWT from the token passed in the request:

```
token, err = jwt.ParseWithClaims(auth, claims, config.keyFunc)
    if err == nil && token.Valid {
        // Store user information from token into context.
        c.Set(config.ContextKey, token)
        return next(c)
    }
```

This allows our handlers to remain completely ignorant of the fact that we need to perform authentication, causing our routes to be less complex and easier to read.

Summary

Throughout this chapter, we have learned about middleware and how to implement and use middleware within the Echo framework. Middleware serves as a means to minimize duplication within your handler code by abstracting common functionality out of the handlers. By using middleware, your code will become more streamlined and easier to maintain as changes can be made without touching every handler within your web application. This means that your web application can remain ignorant to the functionality that the middleware provides. This chapter also outlines a variety of middleware functions that come with the Echo framework that have been contributed to by the community.

The next chapter will dive into details mentioned within this chapter of request data binding. We will also cover the `echo.Context` primitive, which allows us to pass application context from the Echo framework through middleware functionality, all the way to the end handler code.

5
Utilizing the Request Context and Data Bindings

As the saying goes, "context is everything" and within the Echo framework, everything is accessible through the request context. Context implementation within Echo allows for the simplification of otherwise difficult information passing, as well as state transference through middleware and handlers. Within Echo, we can think of the `echo.Context` type as a representation of the request itself and reference its methods in order to retrieve any information about the incoming request.

Along with context, converting the serialized representation of a request payload data into a structure that is usable within an application is of paramount concern for a web application. Echo provides a very helpful capability that will handle the deserialization of the request payload into a structure for use within your handlers. This allows the developer to create custom data structures within the web application, and by using the `context.Bind` method, convert the request into the developer-defined data structure.

Within web applications, where there is a request, there should be a response. This chapter will also cover the built-in capabilities of Echo's response rendering. These capabilities allow the developer to send the response HTTP code and a custom data structure representing the response payload as parameters. Echo then serializes this data structure into the wire format which is applicable for the response payload and writes the response to the `http.ResponseWriter` implementation.

By the end of this chapter, you will have learned about how Echo's context is a low cost abstraction that provides value to your application. These abstractions allow developers to focus on the business logic of the application instead of re-inventing the wheel for serialization and deserialization of data. Within this chapter, we will dive into the following topics, and show you how to implement these solutions within the Echo framework:

- Maintaining the context through middleware and handlers
- Extending the context interface with custom implementations

- Request data binding capabilities
- Response rendering capabilities

We will conclude this chapter with some example code that will show best practices for working with custom context implementations, as well as request data binding and response rendering using the Echo framework.

Technical requirements

You will be required to know Go programming language, also basics of web application framework. You will also need to install Git, in order use the Git repository of this book. And finally, ability to develop with an IDE on the command line.

The code files of this chapter can be found on GitHub:
https://github.com/PacktPublishing/Echo-Essentials/tree/master/chapter5

Check out the following video to see the code in action:
https://goo.gl/3gDXrq

Maintaining context

Throughout early Go web application development, there was much contention surrounding how to weave together context when chaining handler function calls together. If we examine the standard library `http.HandlerFunc` definition, `type HandlerFunc func(ResponseWriter, *Request)`, this type is not conducive for building a chained middleware scheme, or calling other request handlers from within handlers whatsoever. This is because of the two different parameters, `http.ResponseWriter` and `*http.Request`. The `http.ResponseWriter` is an interface that is designed primarily to write a sequence of bytes back to the caller, whereas the second parameter, the `*http.Request`, is a pointer to the data structure that represents the request.

Prior to Go 1.7, there was no mechanism in place within the `http.Request` type to store extra information to keep the state from one nested handler function call to the next. This absence of a means of keeping context, or extra information created from the request in prior handlers, caused web application handlers to grow very large, as they were effectively responsible for handling all of the business logic that is commonly implemented in a middleware pipeline.

This lack of being able to keep the context within the confines of the standard library lead to a few different solutions. The three primary solutions that were used are as follows:

- Frameworks that use a single global mapping of requests to request context data
- Frameworks that implement a new function signature for web handlers that include a context parameter
- Frameworks that hid the metadata within the request data structure

Each of these solutions are discussed in the following subsections.

Globally requesting context mapping

Within a global request to request a context mapping solution, there is a single data structure in which you can look up the context for a request. The most popular implementation of this can be found within the Gorilla web toolkit, which can be found here: https://github.com/gorilla/context.

At a very high level, this code creates a single `map[*http.Request]map[interface{}]interface{}` global variable, which is available through the helper `Get` and `Set` functions. When used, if you `'Set'` some contextual variable, the code will create a new `map[interface{}]interface{}`, and uses the request pointer of the request the contextual information belongs to as a map key in the global map, the value of which would be the newly created `map[interface{}]interface{}`. Then, the set call would add the key/value pair to the newly created `map[interface{}]interface{}`:

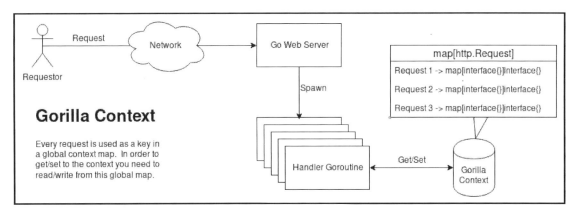

This design is not optimal due to the memory allocations that need to be performed for every single request. Each request that comes in needs to be inserted into this map. A new map needs to also be allocated to hold the contextual information, too. As we have already discussed, the Go web server creates a new `goroutine` for every single request that comes into the server. There could be potentially hundreds or thousands of concurrent `goroutines` handling requests within a web server. With all of these `goroutines`, there would be a lot of contention to read from and write to this global map. Moreover, within the design, unless you explicitly clear the context map entries, there is a potential memory leak situation, which is clear from the documentation.

The new handler function type

Prior to Go 1., the request data structure in the standard library did not include any form of modifiable context structure. Due to this limitation in the standard library, it makes sense that many frameworks decided that the standard library definition of what a handler did not offer needed flexibility. That being the case, these frameworks developed their own concepts of context, and changed their handler function type to pass in a context instead. In the following snippet, you can see the differences between these handler types, where the Echo handler function type has a context parameter, while the standard library does not:

```
type HandlerFunc func(ResponseWriter, *Request) // http handler function type
type HandlerFunc func(Context) error // Echo handler function type
```

Web frameworks that created a context type and a new `HandlerFunc` definition that took the context type as a parameter had a few small concerns to address. Firstly, the portability of the handler code to switch from one web framework to another dramatically drops. Effectively, you have vendor lock-in because in order to switch to a new web framework, you would have to refactor all of your handlers. Secondly, the context type used as the parameter would need to include both the request and the response structures, as well as provide an interface to add contextual data. Looking at the current Echo context interface definition, you can see that the context implementation needs to implement 53 methods. The context literally has everything including the kitchen sink.

You might be wondering, if Echo needs to create a new context for every single request, how can Echo be a low-cost abstraction? Echo achieves this by implementing a `sync.Pool` context, which is a set of temporary instances that may be saved and retrieved. With this capability, every time Echo needs a request context to be created, it actually goes to the pool and draws an existing context instance and re-uses it. Other frameworks do not do this, and suffer from new context instance allocations for every request that comes into their web application:

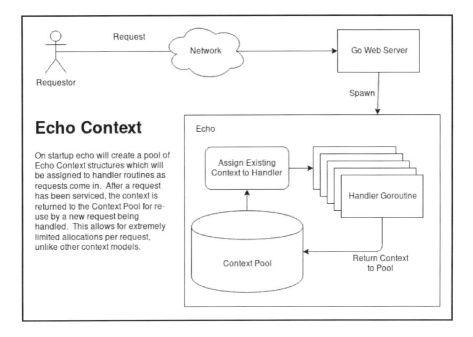

The context is central to application development within Echo, as you can see based on the handler function signature. From the context structure, you have access to the original request structure, response writer, as well as a shared request, processing state from upstream middleware functions.

Hiding context within a request

A third clever mechanism for passing contextual state to handlers from the web application framework or middleware is to hide the context within the request itself. Since the request contains dynamic map information such as request headers and form key/value pairs, it is fairly easy to embed new information into this existing structure.

A good example of this is the Vestigo URL Router: https://github.com/husobee/vestigo. This standalone URL router actually hides the request URL parameter names and values within form fields on the request structure itself. This allows the developer to access the contextual framework's supplied information, in this case, the URL parameter names and values, without the need to use a central map or use a modified function signature. What is striking about this design is that the developer using this web application framework will be able to get all of the URL parameters from the router within their application handlers without subscribing to a modified application handler function signature.

Post Go 1.7

Due to the release of Go 1.7, the standard library now offers context implementation within the request data structure itself. This means that one no longer has to choose between one of the prior options for passing the context from handler to handler when building a web framework, as that context is now always present on the request itself. Granted, this context is a little more of a bare bones lightweight context, but it does support cancellation and is used elsewhere.

Echo context

The `echo.Context` interface defines the following methods which provide the developer with helper functions to retrieve various information about the request that is made, as well as manipulate the state of the context. The following is a shortened list of important methods available on the context, along with a short description of what each method provides:

- `Param(name string) string`:
    - Returns the value of the URL parameter that is mapped to by `name`
    - This is the primary interface by which you retrieve URL parameters within your handler and middleware functions
    - The `name` parameter provided to this function is the string that was used within the routing path definition
- `QueryParam(name string) string`:
    - Returns the value of the URL query parameter that is mapped to by `name`
    - This allows you to access the query parameter by parameter name instead of using the standard library's `http.Request` URL to access the `Query` method
    - Designed as a helper function to access query string parameters
- `FormValue(name string) string`:
    - Returns the value of the form payload parameter that is mapped to by `name`
    - This will return the value of a submitted form's attribute defined by `name`

- `FormFile(name string) (*multipart.FileHeader, error)`:
  - Returns the multi-part form file that is mapped to by `name`
- `Cookie(name string) (*http.Cookie, error)`:
  - Returns the cookie that is mapped to by `name` from the request
- `SetCookie(cookie *http.Cookie)`:
  - Adds a `Set-Cookie` response header, which is useful for setting cookie values
- `Get(key string) interface{}`:
  - Retrieves an arbitrary value from the context that is mapped to by key
  - This is useful for retrieving the state that was set by middleware and other handler functions
- `Set(key string, val interface{})`:
  - Sets an arbitrary key/value pair on the context
  - This is useful for setting the state for use in future middleware or handlers
- `Handler() HandlerFunc`:
  - Returns the handler function found in the router
  - This is the actual function that the Echo framework is going to perform based on the routing results
- `Logger() Logger`:
  - This will return an instance of the Echo logger
  - With this, you will be able to use the built-in Echo logging infrastructure to create logs

The remaining functionality of the `echo.Context` primarily revolves around input binding and validation of request payloads, as well as rendering capabilities provided by Echo. These topics will be defined in-depth in the following sections of this chapter. It is important to remember when developing an application with the Echo framework that context is a central primitive of the framework, which will increase your efficiency in development.

As you can see, the context is truly everything within the Echo framework. The contextual information provided to the middleware and handlers allows for state to be created and passed along the request processing pipeline through middleware and handler functions.

Request binding

Within the context interface in the Echo framework, there is a method called `Bind`, which will perform request payload binding. The following is the definition of the function:

```
// Bind binds the request body into provided type `i`. The default binder
// does it based on Content-Type header.
Bind(i interface{}) error
```

In essence, the `Context.Bind` function takes the payload and `Content-Type` header from the HTTP request, and converts it into any structure defined by the passed in `i interface{}` function parameter. This is a very handy feature of the web application framework as it removes a lot of the coding required by the developer to interpret the request payload themselves. Instead of having to perform deserialization of the HTTP request body yourself, Echo will perform this for you. The following is an example handler that uses the `Bind` function call, which is located at `$GOPATH/src/github.com/PacktPublishing/Echo-Essentials/chapter5/handlers/login.go`:

```
func Login(c echo.Context) error {
        resp := renderings.LoginResponse{}
        lr := new(bindings.LoginRequest)

        if err := c.Bind(lr); err != nil {
                resp.Success = false
                resp.Message = "Unable to bind request for login"
                return c.JSON(http.StatusBadRequest, resp)
        }
        // ...
```

As you can see in the preceding example, we are creating a new `*bindings.LoginRequest` in our project's `$GOPATH/src/github.com/PacktPublishing/Echo-Essentials/chapter5/handlers/login.go` file, which is the object we want to deserialize from the request payload. The following is the structure of `$GOPATH/src/github.com/PacktPublishing/Echo-Essentials/chapter5/bindings/login.go`:

```
type LoginRequest struct {
        Username string `json:"username"`
        Password string `json:"password"`
}
```

Chapter 5

The `bindings.LoginRequest` structure is comprised of two attributes, a `Username` and a `Password`, which in `json` form are defined as `username` and `password` from the struct tag definitions we have outlined in the structure. When we perform a call to our login handler with the following curl command, the `lr` variable will be populated:

```
curl -XPOST -H"Content-Type: application/json" localhost:8080/login -d'{"username":"test", "password":"test"}' -D -
```

Notice the `Content-Type: application/json` request header we have specified. The following is an example of a valid `curl` command that uses XML instead of JSON:

```
curl -XPOST -H"Content-Type: application/xml" localhost:8080/login -d'<LoginRequest><Username>test</Username><Password>test</Password></LoginRequest>' -D -
```

Echo comes with built-in content-type awareness for the following content types: `application/json`, `application/xml`, and `application/x-www-form-urlencoded`. As you can see, we were able to create our application without regard to the actual wire encoding of the request. The following is an illustration of the preceding example:

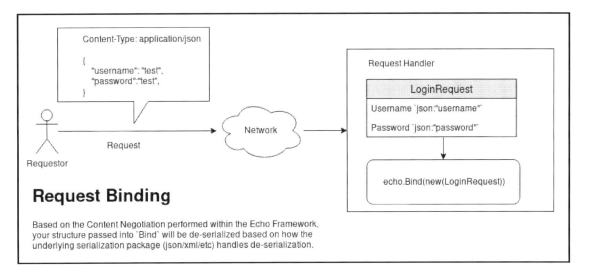

Utilizing the Request Context and Data Bindings

This way, we will be able to support more content types without any additional code out of the box. Content negotiation is valuable to you as an API developer as it makes your application more accessible. By offering your API in multiple content types, you open up your API to more potential integration.

With request binding capabilities, Echo comes out of the box with request binding validation. Request binding validation as a feature of a web application framework gives you the ability to create a common scheme by which all of your API request inputs are validated so that you do not have to clutter your application handler functions with the minutia of how inputs are going to be validated. With the Context.Validate functionality, which is realized in the following example, we are able to create validation on our request input. In order to create a validation scheme where we can clearly define validation code as a method on our request input structures, we first we need to set up an Echo Validator and register it with the Echo framework, which is done by implementing the Validator interface in $GOPATH/src/github.com/PacktPublishing/Echo-Essentials/chapter5/bindings/common.go, as shown in the following code snippet:

```
type Validatable interface {
        Validate() error
}

var ErrNotValidatable = errors.New("Type is not validatable")

type Validator struct{}

func (v *Validator) Validate(i interface{}) error {
        if validatable, ok := i.(Validatable); ok {
                return validatable.Validate()
        }
        return ErrNotValidatable
}
```

As seen in the preceding code, our custom Validator structure must implement a Validate method that takes an interface{} as a parameter, which represents the structure to which we have bound our input. Since our preferred design keeps the validation code as close to the structure to which it is validating, our solution presented in this chapter's sample code needs to be as generic as possible.

This particular custom Validator is type checking that the input implements the Validatable interface, and then runs Validate on that type. By creating this new Validatable interface in our project, any structure that has a method called Validate that returns an error type as the response can be fed into the Validator.Validate function. This provides a very slick abstraction that will help organize your input bindings better, and make validation much easier for your project. In order for our request type to implement the Validatable interface, we will update our login bindings in $GOPATH/src/github.com/PacktPublishing/Echo-Essentials/chapter5/bindings/login.go to resemble the following:

```
package bindings

type LoginRequest struct {
        Username string `json:"username"`
        Password string `json:"password"`
}

func (lr *LoginRequest) Validate() error {
        errs := new(RequestErrors)
        if lr.Username == "" {
                errs.Append(ErrUsernameEmpty)
        }
        if lr.Password == "" {
                errs.Append(ErrPasswordEmpty)
        }
        if errs.Len() == 0 {
                return nil
        }
        return errs
}
```

Within the preceding example code, you can clearly see that our LoginRequest type now implements the Validatable interface because it has a Validate function that returns an error. Each input binding structure you create for your project will now clearly show how that input structure is validated right next to the structure definition itself. This makes the code much cleaner than if you were to implement this validation code in your handlers each time you bind your request data to a structure.

Utilizing the Request Context and Data Bindings

All we need to do now is to set Echo to use our custom `Validator` in `$GOPATH/src/github.com/PacktPublishing/Echo-Essentials/chapter5/cmd/service/main.go`, as shown in the following code:

```
func main() {
        // create a new echo instance
        e := echo.New()
        e.Logger.SetLevel(log.INFO)
        e.Validator = new(bindings.Validator)

        //...
```

The preceding example shows that by merely setting the `Validator` attribute on the Echo instance to our new `Validator` structure, we are able to use the validation capabilities built into the Echo Context to validate inputs within our request handler code. At this point, we are ready to use the `Context.Validate` method in our handler to validate that our input is valid in `handlers/login.go`, which will run our binding's validate function that we defined previously. We will insert our validation after our binding occurs, as follows:

```
//...
        if err := c.Bind(lr); err != nil {
                resp.Success = false
                resp.Message = "Unable to bind request for login"
                return c.JSON(http.StatusBadRequest, resp)
        }

        if err := c.Validate(lr); err != nil {
                resp.Success = false
                resp.Message = err.Error()
                return c.JSON(http.StatusBadRequest, resp)
        }
//...
```

By using the binding and validation capabilities within Echo, we save time and effort in our application development process. There is no need to worry about the deserialization of the wire format of the request payload, and we can create structure in our code for following best practices for the validation of inputs. Within the preceding handler code, we used the `Context.Bind` method to read our inputs into the request structure. Afterward, we immediately called `Context.Validate` and passed in the structure we just bound to perform validation on the structure.

Response rendering

As mentioned in `Chapter 1`, *Understanding HTTP, Go, and Echo*, the primary purpose of a web application is to take in a request, and render a response to the caller. Fortunately for us, Echo has a multitude of ways we can render responses back to callers. The Echo `Context` has the following helpers that can be used to render responses, so that you as a developer will not need to serialize the response data yourself:

```
HTML(code int, html string) error
HTMLBlob(code int, b []byte) error
String(code int, s string) error
JSON(code int, i interface{}) error
JSONPretty(code int, i interface{}, indent string) error
JSONBlob(code int, b []byte) error
JSONP(code int, callback string, i interface{}) error
JSONPBlob(code int, callback string, b []byte) error
XML(code int, i interface{}) error
XMLPretty(code int, i interface{}, indent string) error
XMLBlob(code int, b []byte) error
Blob(code int, contentType string, b []byte) error
Stream(code int, contentType string, r io.Reader) error
File(file string) error
Attachment(file string, name string) error
Inline(file string, name string) error
NoContent(code int) error
Redirect(code int, url string) error
```

Each of the preceding `Context` methods allow the developer to specify the particular content type encoding that is needed for the response of the web application. If your API is returning JSON, for example, you should use the `Context.JSON` method to render your structure to the caller.

How this works is very simple: when you call `context.JSON`, behind the scenes, Echo takes the first parameter `code` and writes that status code to the `ResponseWriter`. After the status and headers have been written, Echo then takes the `interface{}` structure that you pass as the second parameter, serializes said structure to JSON encoding, and then performs a `ResponseWriter.Write` with the resultant encoded JSON.

The following is an example from our `$GOPATH/src/github.com/PacktPublishing/Echo-Essentials/chapter5/handlers/login.go` code, where we return a JSON representation of the response structure:

```
return c.JSON(http.StatusOK, resp)
```

Utilizing the Request Context and Data Bindings

By calling the JSON method and specifying a response status code, and our `renderings.LoginResponse` structure as parameters, Echo will serialize our `renderings.LoginResponse` to JSON and write the response directly to the `http.ResponseWriter`, which means that the developer does not have to worry about encoding:

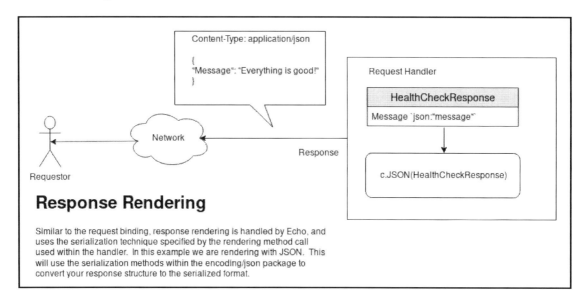

echo.Response

In the previous subsection, we saw an extremely high level developer view of interacting with Echo's response capabilities using the simple rendering capabilities within the context. Within this subsection, we will dive a bit deeper into how you can use Echo's Response capabilities to improve your API with customization. Within the context, there is a `Response` method that when called will return an `echo.Response` structure by which you can manipulate the underlying response. The following is the structure defined within Echo for `echo.Response`:

```
type (
  // Response wraps an http.ResponseWriter and implements its interface to be used
  // by an HTTP handler to construct an HTTP response.
  // See: https://golang.org/pkg/net/http/#ResponseWriter
  Response struct {
    echo          *Echo
```

```
        beforeFuncs []func()
        afterFuncs  []func()
        Writer      http.ResponseWriter
        Status      int
        Size        int64
        Committed   bool
    }
)
```

As seen in the preceding code, the `echo.Response` structure contains an array of `beforeFuncs` and `afterFuncs`, an `http.ResponseWriter` and a `Status`, which are of particular interest to us. The `http.ResponseWriter` is, as you may recall, given to Echo for every request that comes into the server.

Let's say, for example, it might be beneficial to add various response HTTP headers to the response. By using the `Response` structure, you can add response headers to your handler's response easily, as seen here: `ctx.Response().Header().Add("X-My-Header":"ValueOfHeader")`. Echo's `Response` structure has a helper method, `Header`, that wraps the `http.ResponseWriter` structure's `Header` method. In the preceding example, by manipulating the `Header`, you are changing the headers that the underlying `http.ResponseWriter` contains.

Similarly, when you perform `Response.WriteHeader` or `Response.Write` method calls, you are in fact calling a wrapper around the `http.ResponseWriter` structure, which can be seen in the following code:

```
// WriteHeader sends an HTTP response header with status code. If
WriteHeader is
// not called explicitly, the first call to Write will trigger an implicit
// WriteHeader(http.StatusOK). Thus explicit calls to WriteHeader are
mainly
// used to send error codes.
func (r *Response) WriteHeader(code int) {
  if r.Committed {
    r.echo.Logger.Warn("response already committed")
    return
  }
  for _, fn := range r.beforeFuncs {
    fn()
  }
  r.Status = code
  r.Writer.WriteHeader(code)
  r.Committed = true
}
```

Utilizing the Request Context and Data Bindings

In the following code snippet, you can see the `Write` wrapper from the Echo Framework:

```
// Write writes the data to the connection as part of an HTTP reply.
func (r *Response) Write(b []byte) (n int, err error) {
  if !r.Committed {
    r.WriteHeader(http.StatusOK)
  }
  n, err = r.Writer.Write(b)
  r.Size += int64(n)
  for _, fn := range r.afterFuncs {
    fn()
  }
  return
}
```

The Echo response structure allows you to access every aspect of the response you will be sending to the caller, which makes response rendering very simple and powerful. Alluded to earlier, Echo also comes with `beforeFunc` and `afterFunc` attributes, which are before response functions and after response functions. You are able to add pre-response and post-response functionality through the `Response.Before` and `Response.After` method calls. You would use this capability in the event you need something to happen before you write, or after your finish writing a response. I believe a good example of this would be in the event that you want to perform state cleanup after your response.

Summary

Within this chapter, we have covered quite a few important aspects of the Echo framework. These aspects include context, request binding, and response rendering. We have compared and contrasted the difficulties in designing a web framework that will allow us to abstract business logic into middleware by passing the context from one handler function to the next in the processing chain. We also discovered the key features of the Echo Context, as well as the useful features for binding and validating of data, as well as rendering responses.

The next chapter will be dedicated to logging and error handling capabilities within the Echo framework. We will cover how best to organize your code to take advantage of logging. We will also explain how errors are handled within Echo.

6
Performing Logging and Error Handling

Logging and error handling in a web application drastically aids in the troubleshooting of the application by operations team members. Reliable and deterministic error handling is essential to creating robust and reliable applications. The ability to provide team members the relevant information about the state of the running service is also important. By providing logging and tracing patterns within your service, you will be able to quickly isolate what is happening based on the logged information.

So much time is dedicated in application development to working out the functionality of the success case. This makes sense, as the service or application needs to function in the first place. It is very often easy to overlook the not-so-successful cases. By not handling errors well, your application will likely not be resilient, or fail with grace.

In this chapter, we will be covering two often overlooked, but critically important, aspects of web application development. We will start by looking at how logging can be accomplished within the confines of the Echo framework. We will then look at how we can use Echo to capture the `handler` function and middleware errors before they are broadcast to the consumers of your service. In this chapter, we will explore the following topics:

- Logging
  - Echo's Logger interface, and how to extend the logger
  - Typical use cases of the logger within your application
  - Log levels and the appropriate use of log levels.
  - Introducing to the logging middleware
- Error handling
  - The error-handling function and capabilities built into Echo
  - How to customize error handling with Echo

Technical requirements

You will be required to know Go programming language, also basics of web application framework. You will also need to install Git, in order use the Git repository of this book. And finally, ability to develop with an IDE on the command line.

The code files of this chapter can be found on GitHub:
https://github.com/PacktPublishing/Echo-Essentials/tree/master/chapter6

Check out the following video to see the code in action:
https://goo.gl/owjFvG

Logging

It is very often the case that you will need to log events within your web application. Echo provides a simple mechanism by which the developer can access the logger through the `echo.Context` by calling the `Logger` method. When you instantiate the Echo framework, a logger can be set, which is the same logger that you will be able to access from the context. The following code can be used to access the logger in your application handler, giving you the ability to write logs with various log levels, as shown in the following code. The code is taken from `$GOPATH/src/github.com/PacktPublishing/Echo-Essentials/chapter6/handlers/health_check.go`:

```go
// HealthCheck - Health Check Handler
func HealthCheck(c echo.Context) error {
    if reqID, ok := c.Get(middlewares.RequestIDContextKey).(uuid.UUID); ok {
        c.Logger().Debugf("RequestID: %s", reqID.String())
    }
    resp := renderings.HealthCheckResponse{
        Message: "Everything is good!",
    }
    return c.JSON(http.StatusOK, resp)
}
```

As you can see from the preceding simple code, we are able to call the `c.Logger()` function, which will return the `Logger` implementation from the `echo.Context` object we are passed in our `handler` function. From there, in this code, we call the `Debugf` function, which will log a debug log entry.

Echo's Logger interface

Echo provides us with a `Logger` interface, which facilitates logging both within Echo itself and within this mechanism, which will allow you to access this logger from within your middleware and application handlers. The `echo.Logger` interface is extremely flexible. The default logger that Echo uses is the `labstack/gommon/log` logger defined within the `https://github.com/labstack/gommon/` repository, but, if you so choose, you can insert your own custom logging by merely implementing the `Logger` interface. The following is a full listing of the capabilities of the `Logger` interface, which, when implemented, will give the following capabilities:

```
type Logger interface {
    Output() io.Writer
    SetOutput(w io.Writer)
    Prefix() string
    SetPrefix(p string)
    Level() log.Lvl
    SetLevel(v log.Lvl)
    Print(i ...interface{})
    Printf(format string, args ...interface{})
    Printj(j log.JSON)
    Debug(i ...interface{})
    Debugf(format string, args ...interface{})
    Debugj(j log.JSON)
    Info(i ...interface{})
    Infof(format string, args ...interface{})
    Infoj(j log.JSON)
    Warn(i ...interface{})
    Warnf(format string, args ...interface{})
    Warnj(j log.JSON)
    Error(i ...interface{})
    Errorf(format string, args ...interface{})
    Errorj(j log.JSON)
    Fatal(i ...interface{})
    Fatalj(j log.JSON)
    Fatalf(format string, args ...interface{})
    Panic(i ...interface{})
    Panicj(j log.JSON)
    Panicf(format string, args ...interface{})
}
```

As you can see, `echo.Logger` implementations will provide six log-level logging functions: `Debug`, `Info`, `Warn`, `Error`, `Fatal`, and `Panic`. The logger also provides a `Print`, `Printf`, and `Printj` capability if the developer does not want to specify the log level and just wants to have the log message output regardless of the log level. Each level provides a plain log message, a formatted log message, and a JSON implementation of logging messages. This gives the developer the flexibility to provide log messages as strings, formatted strings, or a structured logging, such as JSON.

As you can see in the preceding interface, the nonformatted log method calls allow the developer to specify a variadic parameter list to pass in any type of object they wish, which will result in the printing of a list of parameters that are passed in their string representation. For the formatted log methods, the format string is used together with the variadic parameters to populate the log message in the format specified by the developer. The JSON log methods are marshalled with the encodings/json standard library marshalling facilities.

The `Logger` interface also ensures that implementations implement to `SetOutput`, `SetPrefix`, and `SetLevel` as well. These methods allow the developer to specify where and how the logging output is to be written, set any prefix that the logs should be prefixed with, and set the application logging level (`debug`, `info`, `warn`, `error`, `fatal`, `panic`). This is very helpful for our web application development as we are able to change the log level within the application, as shown in the following code, which is in our `$GOPATH/src/github.com/PacktPublishing/Echo-Essentials/chapter6/cmd/service/main.go` file:

```
func main() {
        // create a new echo instance
        e := echo.New()
        e.Logger.SetLevel(log.DEBUG)
        e.Validator = new(bindings.Validator)
```

As you can see in the preceding example, we are able to set the Echo `Logger` to a log level of `log.DEBUG`, thereby allowing our application to log all messages at the debug level.

Log levels

Though they are very common in web application development, it will be beneficial to review the various log levels. During application development, developers either log too much or too little, which leads to problems. It is important to log when appropriate. It may not be appropriate to log various data-structure-specific information in a higher log level, as it might not be appropriate to log important error messages in a lower log level. Information leakage is also important, a prime example of which would be accidentally logging secrets from the application to the logging facilities.

The debug level can be thought of as a level of logging that might be useful for a developer when troubleshooting how an application works. Developers often end up merely putting every log entry they emit in the debug level. This is not a wise idea, as in production environments, you typically do not want the debug logs to spew for the entirety of the application run. Operations will not usually run an application in a production that is running at a debug log level, and therefore, if you use debug too liberally, it is possible for important information to not be logged when exceptional issues arise.

The info level is primarily used as a level to log information that does not report an error, but which is useful for operational purposes. Typical examples of good info-level logging would be client connection information. Very often, this information, such as the remote address connection, the time taken to serve the request method, and the full path requested are valuable bits of information. This information could be used by operations for debugging or load information, and should be logged at the info level. Very typically, the info level is where production logging will be set in order to avoid capturing all of the verbosity of a debug log level.

The warn level is typically used to explain that a recoverable error was encountered that the system has since recovered from, but that someone should probably look into the issue. Since warn is a higher level than info, if you have your log level set at info, warn messages will be emitted too. These bits of information are very valuable to operations teams, as the teams can get an idea of what is happening within your application.

The error level is used when there is an application error that the system could recover from, and which needs to be investigated. The error log level is higher than the warn log level, and will be emitted when the log level is higher than warn.

The fatal level is used when the application has encountered an error from which there is no recovery, and the application will stop. The panic level is used when the application cannot continue and needs to panic, causing the application to stop. Typical use cases for the `Logger.Fatal` and `Logger.Panic` methods are when your web application is unable to start for some reason, such as if it is impossible to connect to a database on startup, or the application is unable to bind to the port.

Logger middleware

Echo comes with a community developed logger middleware that you are able to use within your web application. This middleware takes every request received by the application and logs metadata about the connection. Items logged include the timestamp, request method, request path, and the duration of the request. In order to implement this helpful middleware within your application, you can use the `echo.Use` method on the Echo framework instance, as seen in the following code, which is taken from `$GOPATH/src/github.com/PacktPublishing/Echo-Essentials/chapter6/cmd/service/main.go`:

```
e.Use(middleware.Logger())
```

By using the preceding middleware, you will get the following log messages for each request that comes into your server. You will notice that within this log message we get the timestamp, the remote IP address, host, method, and URI. We also get information about how the request was processed, including the time taken to complete the request (latency), the number of bytes sent from the server, and the response status code:

```
{"time":"2018-03-27T22:09:44.084450941-04:00","id":"","remote_ip":"::1","host":"localhost:8080","method":"GET","uri":"/health-check","status":200,"latency":424727,"latency_human":"424.727µs","bytes_in":0,"bytes_out":33}
```

Error handling

As mentioned in the Go language blog *Error handling and Go*, error handling is important: "The language's design and conventions encourage you to explicitly check for errors where they occur (as distinct from the convention in other languages of throwing exceptions and sometimes catching them)". Within the Echo framework, you may have noticed that every single handler function returns an error. In the following code, we will explore what happens when a handler returns an error. In this case, we will make a new handler in `$GOPATH/src/github.com/PacktPublishing/Echo-Essentials/chapter6/handlers/err.go`, which looks like the following:

```
package handlers

import (
        "errors"

        "github.com/labstack/echo"
)

// Error - Example Error Handler
func Error(c echo.Context) error {
        return errors.New("failure!")
}
```

When we perform a web service call on the endpoint that routes to this `handler` code, we get the following:

```
curl localhost:8080/error -D -
HTTP/1.1 500 Internal Server Error
Content-Type: application/json; charset=UTF-8
Date: Wed, 28 Mar 2018 02:22:04 GMT
Content-Length: 35

{"message":"Internal Server Error"}
```

Performing Logging and Error Handling

Echo is actually interpreting the error we are returning from our `handler`, and sending an `Internal Server Error` back to the caller. This is done with the `Echo.HTTPErrorHandler` method definition on the Echo instance. This error handler takes in an error as a parameter and a context parameter, and performs the conversion from the error from the `handler` or middleware and converts it to a legitimate response for the user. Within Echo, this method is completely replaceable. By default, it uses the `echo.DefaultHTTPErrorHandler`, as can be seen at https://github.com/labstack/echo/blob/60f88a7a1c4beaf04b6f9254c8d72b45a2ab161e/echo.go#L317:

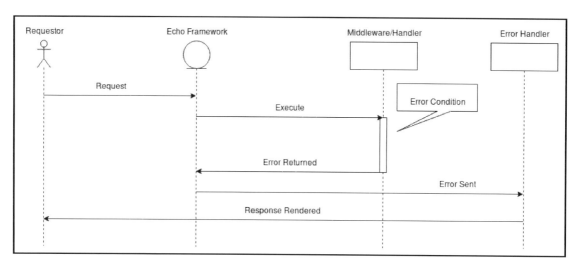

With this functionality, you will be able to replace the default error functionality and truly handle errors within your application appropriately. An example of a custom error handler can be seen in the following code:

```
func myHTTPErrorHandler(err error, c echo.Context) {
    code := http.StatusInternalServerError
    if httpErr, ok := err.(*echo.HTTPError); ok {
        code = httpErr.Code
    }
    c.String
}

e.HTTPErrorHandler = myHTTPErrorHandler
```

Even if you do not want to go through the trouble of managing your own custom error type, so long as you return an `echo.HTTPError` that is fully populated with a status code and message, the `echo.DefaultHTTPErrorHandler` will take care of your response to the caller appropriately. It will check the error's type in the `DefaultHTTPErrorHandler`, and if it is of the `echo.HTTPError` type, Echo will apply the status code and message that was specified within the error definition.

Handling application panics

Application panics are unfortunate, but how you recover from an application panic is very important. Echo comes with a `Recover` middleware that is actually able to catch application panics using the Go `recover` built-n function to catch an application panic. This is possible because, if you recall, middleware functions effectively just wrap our handler functions. Since that is the case, the `Recover` middleware is able to do the following:

```
defer func() {
        if r := recover(); r != nil {
            //...
        }
    }()
```

With the preceding code in place, any application panic that befalls a running request handling `goroutine` will be caught. I strongly recommend reading the *Go blog Defer, Panic and Recover* for more information on how this built-in function works. The following diagram explains what Echo is able to do to catch panics and recover gracefully. If a panic is encountered within the handler function, or any nested middleware, the `Recover` middleware will catch the panic and return a generic error to the Echo framework, which will cause Echo to respond to the caller with the default error handler, which we discussed earlier in this chapter:

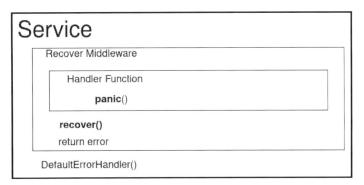

The consequence of not recovering from an application panic could be very embarrassing, as the consumers of your service will get a full stack trace of your application as the response. I would strongly recommend always wrapping your application in the `Recover` middleware just in case you have any kind of application panic within your service.

Summary

In conclusion, logging and error handling within an Echo-based web application allows the developer a mechanism to make their applications more reliable and resilient. This will lead to fewer problems at deployment time, as well as a decreased need for developer interaction at operations time. In this chapter, we have shown you how to effectively use the logging capabilities in Echo to standardize how logging is performed within your web application. We have also looked at how Echo handles error conditions, and the best practices for the propagation of errors through middleware and handler functions.

In `Chapter 7`, *Testing Applications*, we are taking on the elephant in the room by talking about how to test web applications. More often than not, testing web applications is a practice that is generally forgotten or ignored by developers, unfortunately. We will show you how to break down your web application into units that are testable. We will also talk about testing strategies for web application development.

7
Testing Applications

Testing is critical to creating robust applications, and yet testing is very often avoided, or overlooked by developers. I believe part of the reasoning is that companies prioritize application feature speed to market over quality and robust application development. Another reason is that proper automated testing is considered difficult, whereas manual testing of an application is seen as the easier solution.

Within this chapter, we will tackle the problems and solutions of testing applications within Go and more specifically, how we can test our Echo web applications. We start by covering the five primary categories of application testing and then progress into how each type of testing can be accomplished for our example web application. It will be shown how handler and middleware functions can be tested independently of the entire system. You will learn how to mock function calls in order to test various branches of your handlers, as well as point out tools that can help. Finally, we will show how you can perform external and integration testing using Go to build instrumented executable builds.

The entire purpose of testing applications is to prove the code is performing and functioning the way it was designed. Without tests, you will have absolutely no idea what your code is actually doing. Testing is the empirical mechanism by which you can show the business the code functions and provide empirical proof to the business that this application is ready.

This chapter will showcase how to perform various testing of your Go web application. By using the standard library testing facilities for your Go application, you are provided with a framework in which you can create unit tests as well as benchmark tests for your application. By performing some build trickery, you will be shown how to compile a coverage-enabled instrumented executable, for which you can get real solid coverage numbers from your integration testing. You will learn how to unit and benchmark test your handler code, as well as middleware code to find functional and performance problems within your code. By the end of this chapter, you will have a very strong grasp on the importance and functionality of testing your Echo project.

Technical requirements

You will be required to know Go programming language, also basics of web application framework. You will also need to install Git, in order use the Git repository of this book. And finally, ability to develop with an IDE on the command line.

The code files of this chapter can be found on GitHub:
https://github.com/PacktPublishing/Echo-Essentials/tree/master/chapter7

Check out the following video to see the code in action:
https://goo.gl/PtZgpP

Types of testing

Testing in general can be broken into five primary categories:

- Unit testing
- Benchmark testing
- Behavior testing
- Integration testing
- Security testing

Unit testing

Unit testing is a form of testing that is close to the application code itself. Often times, unit test code lives directly adjacent to the feature code within the code base. The goal of unit testing is to provide a quick answer to the question: *Does this unit of code do what I think it should be doing?* This is the first level of testing that is typically performed, as it lives and runs against the lowest unit of functionality.

Benchmark testing

Benchmark testing is critically important in distributed systems' quality assurance. Benchmark testing is testing the speed and throughput capabilities of a segment of code. Commonly found right next to unit tests, benchmark testing can also be performed at the integration level, as well as the unit level. Benchmark testing provides a clear answer on *Does this code/system perform as well as I think it should?*

Behavior testing

Behavior testing can be summed up as *Does this code/system perform and function the way I see my customers using it?* Behavior testing creates a bridge between product owners, customers, and developers, as behavior tests should be understood by all parties so there is no dependency of opinions in how something is supposed to work.

Integration testing

Integration testing, and the related so-called *full-flow* testing, of an application is a gauge of how well your application will integrate with other systems within your environment. For example, let's say we use a database system for storing users login information. How do we know for sure your code handles real data correctly? Within the unit testing level of testing, we may have mocked response data that we know will work with our system. Integration testing is important, and for better or worse, when developers hear the word *testing* they think of integration testing.

Security testing

Security testing, or penetration testing, is often overlooked up until the point that there is a security breach caused by application code. Items of interest tested in this real situation include Cross Site Scripting, SQL and command injection, Cross Origin Resource Sharing, and many others. This testing will prove *Is this application as secure as I think it is?*

Unit testing middleware and handler code

Luckily for developers, unit testing in Go is completely contained within the standard library. In other languages, it is often the case you need to use a third-party library for the creation and running of unit tests. Within Go, the standard library contains all of the tools needed to write, run and analyze unit tests. Within this section, we will learn how to write tests in Go, but also how to use Echo within our tests.

Testing Applications

We will start with the small example test given here, which primarily unit tests our simple /health-check endpoint. To start out, all tests within Go have a very special naming convention. The filename must end with _test.go and must be within the same package, or directory, of the code it is trying to test. Often times in other languages and frameworks, you have the flexibility to create a dedicated test/ directory in order to logically organize functionality versus tests. Within Go, we only have this ability if we are specifically testing only exported functionality. This limits what you are able to test and although possible, this is not practical. Filename and directory location are very important when referencing exported versus non-exported functionality from within a package. With that in mind, we will create the following file, $GOPATH/src/github.com/PacktPublishing/Echo-Essentials/chapter7/handlers/health_check_test.go where we will write a unit test for our health-check handler:

```go
func TestHealthCheck(t *testing.T) {
        e := echo.New()
        e.Pre(middlewares.RequestIDMiddleware)
        e.GET("/health-check", HealthCheck)

        w := httptest.NewRecorder()
        r, _ := http.NewRequest("GET", "/health-check", nil)

        e.ServeHTTP(w, r)

        resp := w.Result()
        if resp.StatusCode != http.StatusOK {
                t.Error("unexpected status code: ", resp.Status)
        }
}
```

In this first part of the test, we need to set up our Echo instance for the test. We also need to add our RequestIDMiddleware that the handler needs to operate correctly and our route. This is very similar to the how the route is added in our main application. After that is set up, we need to create a ResponseRecorder as well as an *http.Request which will mimic what a real request will have in it. Finally, we pass these to our e.ServeHTTP method which will populate the ResponseRecorder with the results from the handler. Next, we validate that the results are what we are expecting to see for this handler function located at $GOPATH/src/github.com/PacktPublishing/Echo-Essentials/chapter7/handlers/health_check_test.go:

```go
            healthCheckResponse := new(renderings.HealthCheckResponse)

            dec := json.NewDecoder(resp.Body)
            err := dec.Decode(healthCheckResponse)
            if err != nil {
```

```
                t.Error("error decoding", err)
        }

        if healthCheckResponse.Message != "Everything is good!" {
                t.Error("invalid response message: ",
healthCheckResponse.Message)
        }
}
```

As with the filename convention, there are also function name semantics that we need to follow for the `go test` tool to figure out what are tests to run. Every single test function needs to be prefixed with the word `Test` and every test needs a signature that takes in, as a parameter, a special pointer to the `testing.T` structure. This `testing.T` structure provides helpful function calls, such as `Fail`, `Log`, and `Error` which you can use in your test to inform the test runner of the status of the test or to log information out of your test to standard out.

As you can see in our example test, we create a properly formatted test function called `TestHealthCheck` and directly within, we set up a new instance of our `echo.Echo` structure. We then add our `/health-check` endpoint, which is handled by the `HealthCheck` handler function, the function which we are looking to test. This is all exactly the same as our main entry point, in that we are instantiating our Echo framework for use within the test. In order to have Echo serve this handler, we need to create an `*http.Request`, which we do with the `http.NewRequest` function, which uses the `GET` HTTP method, and the correct endpoint for our health check.

At this point, we need a way to catch the response from Echo, which is where the `httptest.ResponseRecorder` comes into play. As you recall in our overview of the standard library HTTP facilities, handlers in Go take in as a parameter an `http.ResponseWriter` type, to which you can write a response to the caller. This `httptest.ResponseRecorder` is an implementation of `http.ResponseWriter` which will record the status code, headers, and response body. It also provides helpful functions we will see later in this example to retrieve that data.

After the Echo framework runs the request, we need to start asserting that we get back what we expect from the handler code to the client. We have three things to check for at this point: the correct response status code; the ability to decode the JSON correctly; and the response data matches what we expect from the handler.

With the `httptest.ResponseRecorder`, you can create an `*http.Response` structure by calling `Result()` off of the `httptest.ResponseRecorder`. From the `*http.Response`, we are able to read the status code for our first assertion. Then we can take the `Body` off of the response and feed it into a JSON decoder to validate the JSON is well formed, and finally we can validate the message matches what we expect. When we run this test from the project root as shown, we get the following result:

```
go test -v ./handlers -cover
=== RUN   TestHealthCheck
--- PASS: TestHealthCheck (0.00s)
PASS
coverage: 7.9% of statements
ok      github.com/PacktPublishing/Echo-Essentials/chapter7/handlers
0.006s  coverage: 7.9% of statements
```

As you can see, unit testing in Go is fairly easy, in that you are just writing code that calls the functions you wish to test within the application. Unit testing will provide a lot of value so long as you are able to structure your code in a way that is easy to write tests. Where unit testing becomes difficult is when you write code without a mechanism for abstracting out the integration specific functionality. There are a few mechanisms that can help with these integration specific problems, mocking and monkey patching.

Mocking is useful, and tragically brittle all at the same time. Given that Go provides `interface` types, it is easy to create an interface that defines the particular methods that can be implemented by third-party dependencies. For an example of this, consider the `sql.DB` type. For unit testing, you do not want to have to run a full instance of a SQL database, complete with appropriate schema and fixture data. That would be considered an integration test, as you are at that point of not just testing your code, but also testing a database integration. What if we created an abstraction where we defined our own `DB` interface that had the same function signatures as the `sql.DB` structure? Following is an example from `github.com/PacktPublishing/Echo-Essentials/chapter7/models/mocks.go`:

```
type MockableDB interface {
    Begin() (*sql.Tx, error)
    BeginTx(ctx context.Context, opts *sql.TxOptions) (*sql.Tx, error)
    Close() error
    Conn(ctx context.Context) (*sql.Conn, error)
    Driver() driver.Driver
    Exec(query string, args ...interface{}) (sql.Result, error)
    ExecContext(ctx context.Context, query string, args ...interface{}) (sql.Result, error)
    Ping() error
    PingContext(ctx context.Context) error
```

```
  Prepare(query string) (*sql.Stmt, error)
  PrepareContext(ctx context.Context, query string) (*sql.Stmt, error)
  Query(query string, args ...interface{}) (*sql.Rows, error)
  QueryContext(ctx context.Context, query string, args ...interface{})
(*sql.Rows, error)
  QueryRow(query string, args ...interface{}) *sql.Row
  QueryRowContext(ctx context.Context, query string, args ...interface{})
*sql.Row
  SetConnMaxLifetime(d time.Duration)
  SetMaxIdleConns(n int)
  SetMaxOpenConns(n int)
  Stats() sql.DBStats
}
```

Since we created this interface we are able to create a new structure, MockDB, that implements all of the same functions that sql.DB does, but allows us to mock particular responses, based on criteria passed into it. This would remove the need for running a database for the unit testing all together. The following is an example from the same file of the implementation of a MockDB structure:

```
type MockDB struct {
  mockBegin func() (*sql.Tx, error)
  mockBeginTx func(ctx context.Context, opts *sql.TxOptions) (*sql.Tx,
error)
  mockClose func() error
  mockConn func(ctx context.Context) (*sql.Conn, error)
  mockDriver func() driver.Driver
  mockExec func(query string, args ...interface{}) (sql.Result, error)
  mockExecContext func(ctx context.Context, query string, args
...interface{}) (sql.Result, error)
  mockPing func() error
  mockPingContext func(ctx context.Context) error
  mockPrepare func(query string) (*sql.Stmt, error)
  mockPrepareContext func(ctx context.Context, query string) (*sql.Stmt,
error)
  mockQuery func(query string, args ...interface{}) (*sql.Rows, error)
  mockQueryContext func(ctx context.Context, query string, args
...interface{}) (*sql.Rows, error)
  mockQueryRow func(query string, args ...interface{}) *sql.Row
  mockQueryRowContext func(ctx context.Context, query string, args
...interface{}) *sql.Row
  mockSetConnMaxLifetime func(d time.Duration)
  mockSetMaxIdleConns func(n int)
  mockSetMaxOpenConns func(n int)
  mockStats func() sql.DBStats
}
```

```
func (db *MockDB) Begin() (*sql.Tx, error) {
  if db.mockBegin != nil {
    return db.mockBegin()
  }
  return nil, nil
}
//...
```

The preceding code creates our new `MockDB` structure which implements all of the methods defined by the interface that is mirroring the `sql.DB` type. As you can see by having attributes on the structure where you can override the default behavior of the `MockDB` methods, you can inject whatever functionality you need into this structure. Following is an example of how we can use this scheme within a unit test, taken from `github.com/PacktPublishing/Echo-Essentials/chapter7/models/user_test.go`:

```
func TestGetUserByUsername(t *testing.T) {
  db := &MockDB{
    mockQuery: func(query string, args ...interface{}) (*sql.Rows, error) {
      return nil, errors.New("test query failure!")
    },
  }

  _, err := GetUserByUsername(db, "test")
  if err != nil {
    if errors.Cause(err).Error() != "test query failure!" {
      t.Errorf("incorrect failure expected: %s", err.Error())
    }
  }
}
```

An example of monkey patching in Go is explained in `https://bou.ke/blog/monkey-patching-in-go/` and effectively replaces a function definition during run-time. This is handy when creating tests because you are able to change how the application code functions and mimic particular cases to exercise your code. For example if you want to test out what your code will do if the call to `sql.Open` fails. By using this monkey patching technique your test will replace `sql.Open` with a function you define within your test, that is able to produce the particular error you are wanting to test. One thing to keep in mind is, when you do this technique you will loose the ability to run the tests in parallel as you are really replacing the function.

Take care when mocking to not over mock, or over monkey patch within your tests. It is a great way to increase coverage, but ultimately when you are mocking an integration, you are feeding your code what your code expects to be fed. Just because you have 100% unit test coverage from your mocking, doesn't mean that the integration will work perfectly. Later in this chapter, we talk about integration testing and how to use external testing frameworks to exercise your code.

Benchmark testing web applications

Much like unit testing, benchmark testing within Go is very simple, as Go provides a great abstraction. Also like unit testing, there is a strong convention for naming your benchmark tests. Benchmark tests need to include the word Benchmark at the beginning of the function name. In addition, the parameter expected is the *testing.B type instead of the *testing.T structure. Here is an example in which we benchmark our /health-check endpoint, which can be found in $GOPATH/src/github.com/PacktPublishing/Echo-Essentials/chapter7/handlers/health_check_test.go:

```
func BenchmarkHealthCheck(b *testing.B) {
        e := echo.New()
        e.Pre(middlewares.RequestIDMiddleware)
        e.GET("/health-check", HealthCheck)

        w := httptest.NewRecorder()
        r, _ := http.NewRequest("GET", "/health-check", nil)

        for i := 0; i < b.N; i++ {
                e.ServeHTTP(w, r)
        }
}
```

As seen here, our test starts out very similar to the unit test, we still need to create our Echo instance, and set up our `/health-check` endpoint. We must continue to create a response recorder, as well as a request to be served. Where the benchmark test diverges is the `for` loop. This `for` loop says, for `b.N` perform `e.ServeHTTP`. For the benchmark number of possible tries, run the handler code over and over again. The testing package will run this code within this for loop over and over, and increment `b.N` as it goes, until the testing package is satisfied that the benchmark is completed. This will run this `e.ServeHTTP` continually as fast as it can for a determined period of time. When we run the benchmark test shown next, we will get the amount of time required to perform the action:

```
go test -v ./... -bench Benchmark
=== RUN   TestHealthCheck
--- PASS: TestHealthCheck (0.00s)
goos: linux
goarch: amd64
pkg: github.com/PacktPublishing/Echo-Essentials/chapter7/handlers
BenchmarkHealthCheck-8            300000              5095 ns/op
PASS
ok      github.com/PacktPublishing/Echo-Essentials/chapter7/handlers    1.597s
```

As you can see, the time it took to run the `HealthCheck` handler was 5,095 nanoseconds, and in the 1.597 second run time we were able to perform 300K runs of the `HealthCheck` handler. With this benchmark in place, you will be able to alter your code, and know exactly how your alteration affects the performance of your service.

External behavior and integration testing

As seen, the creation of unit tests and benchmark tests within Go is very simple and intuitive. The built in `go test` command allows various coverage capabilities. A little known capability of the `go test` tool is the ability to specify which packages you wish to generate coverage information about with the `-coverpkg` flag. Armed with this information, we can formulate a `go test` command that will be able to run against the `main` package in our program but collect coverage information about our `handlers` package:

```
go test -coverprofile=cov.txt -coverpkg ./handlers -run TestRunMain ./cmd/service/
```

Chapter 7

The preceding command is saying run tests against the `main` package but collect the coverage information from `handlers` that in turn will use the `cover` tool to instrument the handlers code to keep track of coverage numbers in the `handlers` package. If we take this concept to the next logical step, what happens if we have one test in `cmd/service/main_test.go` that merely runs the main entry point of our web application? For our thought experiment, here are the contents of `cmd/service/main_test.go` followed by the modifications to `$GOPATH/src/github.com/PacktPublishing/Echo-Essentials/chapter7/cmd/service/main_test.go`:

```
package main

import (
        "testing"
)

func TestRunMain(t *testing.T) {
        TestRun = true
        go main()
        <-StopTestServer
        TestRun = false
}
```

Next, you will see how we alter `main.go` to include the `TestRun` variable and the `StopTestServer` channel which are used to tell main that this is a test version of the server, and when to stop processing:

```
var (
        StopTestServer = make(chan bool)
        TestRun        = false
)

func main() {
        //...
        if TestRun {
                e.POST("/stop-test-server", func(ctx echo.Context) error {
                        StopTestServer <- true
                        return nil
                })
        }
        //...
}
```

As you can see within our main application, we flag the addition of a POST handler to the endpoint /stop-test-server that is handled by the anonymous function shown, which merely informs our test when it is time to stop the test server. This may seem silly, but now when we run the following command, the go test command starts up our main function and allows us to run external tests against it, and allows us to externally stop the processing of the tests which show us the coverage information for our handlers package:

```
go test ./cmd/service/ -v -coverpkg ./handlers -coverprofile cov.txt -run=TestRunMain
=== RUN   TestRunMain

   ____    __
  / __/___/ /  ___
 / _// __/ _ \/ _ \
/___/\__/_//_/\___/ v3.2.6
High performance, minimalist Go web framework
https://echo.labstack.com
_____O/_____
                                    O\
⇨ http server started on [::]:8080
```

At this point, you are able to perform HTTP calls against this using external tools, such as curl seen here:

```
curl http://localhost:8080/health-check
{"message":"Everything is good!"}
curl -XPOST http://localhost:8080/stop-test-server
```

After performing these two curl commands, if you look at the output from your test run, you will notice that we get some logging information about the requests performed, as well as finally, the coverage information for our handler functions, which is pasted here:

```
--- PASS: TestRunMain (67.31s)
PASS
coverage: 7.9% of statements in ./handlers
ok      github.com/PacktPublishing/Echo-Essentials/chapter7/cmd/service
67.320s  coverage: 7.9% of statements in ./handlers
```

This capability will present real coverage numbers for our handlers package from external testing. External testing frameworks such as cucumber allow you to perform behavior driven testing with a fully featured framework that is not written in Go. This means you will be able to have team members, such as quality engineers write tests for your service in whatever framework they want to, and still get the coverage numbers for your code. As you can see here, with the coverage tool, you can even drill down and see individual function coverage numbers which can help with coverage reports:

```
go tool cover -func=cov.txt

github.com/PacktPublishing/Echo-Essentials/chapter7/handlers/err.go:10:
Error            0.0%
github.com/PacktPublishing/Echo-Essentials/chapter7/handlers/health-
check.go:13:     HealthCheck     100.0%
github.com/PacktPublishing/Echo-Essentials/chapter7/handlers/login.go:19:
Login            0.0%
github.com/PacktPublishing/Echo-Essentials/chapter7/handlers/logout.go:5:
Logout           0.0%
github.com/PacktPublishing/Echo-Essentials/chapter7/handlers/reminder.go:5:
CreateReminder   0.0%
github.com/PacktPublishing/Echo-Essentials/chapter7/handlers/reminder.go:9:
GetReminder      0.0%
total:
(statements)     7.9%
```

It is fairly easy to see how this could benefit an organization if implemented within a Continuous integration and Continuous Deployment pipeline. Tests do not need to be exclusively written in Go, and you can have real integration tested by running the instrumented test server next to a real database and other integrated systems.

Summary

As you can see, testing can be quite involved, and overwhelming to a developer, but it is currently, with the exception of formal method modeling, the only way to be sure your code is doing what you say it is doing. Empirical analysis on instrumented code can show you each and every line in your code that is "covered" by a test. This coverage information is good and bad. It is good because you have a number which marches forward or backward that you can use as a gauge of how much quality your code has within. It is bad because, just like any other gauge, developers can tweak the coverage numbers without actually increasing quality. By merely running code within the testing framework, the coverage number will increase but if your tests do not have valid assertions and are looking for the right things, the test is bunk. A pragmatic and honest approach to testing is a contract between the company and the developer. If a company demands 100% of the lines of code covered by tests, then the developer will cut corners on the tests to make that number. If the company demands more functionality and less testing, then the quality will obviously suffer. There is a fine balancing act that needs to be achieved based on risk.

Within the next chapter, we will be focusing on content delivery with templates and static content. Typically, this is how the world "sees" your web application, through delivery of content. It will be shown how Echo provides a great mechanism for dynamic and static content rendering.

8
Providing Templates and Static Content

A large portion of web application development involves the rendering of **Hypertext Markup Language** (HTML), as well as other dynamic and static content in order to provide an interface for which the users can interact with an application. Within this chapter, we will explore Echo's capabilities regarding static content delivery and create dynamic content that will be rendered on the server side using templates. We will take an inventory of how Echo can help us with the following tasks:

- Serve static content and files from a particular directory on the server
- Create dynamic templates from any template library
- Interact with the Echo web application from within the templates

With these features at your disposal, you will be able to pull together a functional user experience quickly using server-side rendering of dynamic content. You will also be able to limit your deploy scope by serving files directly from within your web application, as opposed to setting up an independent static content delivery service for your application. Lastly, you will be able to implement a clean content delivery mechanism for your web application.

… *Providing Templates and Static Content*

Technical requirements

You will be required to know Go programming language, also basics of web application framework. You will also need to install Git, in order use the Git repository of this book. And finally, ability to develop with an IDE on the command line.

The code files of this chapter can be found on GitHub:
https://github.com/PacktPublishing/Echo-Essentials/tree/master/chapter8

Check out the following video to see the code in action:
https://goo.gl/BAHuF3

Serving static files

When we talk about static files, we are talking about web application assets that are needed in order to render a working user experience. Static file assets include, but are not limited to, **Cascading Style Sheet** (**CSS**) files, **JavaScript** (**JS**) files, and any other file that a user would need to download in order to render the web application within the browser. Within Echo, we are able to present an interface for the browser to download these assets much in the same way we present new routes within Echo. The following is an example from our project where we are going to present a route called /static/ wherein every request that is made to any resource prefixed with /static/ will be served from a particular directory which is based on the location of the binary executable, in our example the ./static/ directory:

```
e.Static("/static", "static")
```

There are a lot of things happening with this one line, so I will break it down. The e.Static method takes two arguments, a route path expression, which in this case is /static, as well as a location on the filesystem, static. This location on the filesystem must be bound to a directory that is within the current working directory. The route path expression employs Echo's wildcard matching capabilities that we covered in the chapter on routing. In essence, this tells Echo that any request that is prefixed with /static/ will be handled by this static handling functionality.

Of interest, within the implementation in Echo there is also a mechanism by which a developer can specify how to serve just a single file as a particular route. For example, if you wanted to serve a file ./static/index.html whenever a user requested the URL /, you could add the following:

```
e.File("/", "static/index.html")
```

With this line we are telling Echo that any request for / should be responded to with the contents of the file located in ./static/index.html. As you can see, this feature allows for flexibility in how the rendering of static content is performed.

Echo exposes Static method below, which allows us to serve static content on a directory level. As you can see in the following, the Static method takes in a prefix, and a root directory to serve files from:

```
// Static registers a new route with path prefix to serve static files from the
// provided root directory.
func (e *Echo) Static(prefix, root string) *Route {
        if root == "" {
                root = "." // For security we want to restrict to CWD.
        }
        return static(e, prefix, root)
}
```

It is helpful to note that this code will default the root path to the current working directory in the event you pass in an empty string to the Static method. Following is how the static function implements the routing and serving of static content:

```
func static(i i, prefix, root string) *Route {
        h := func(c Context) error {
                p, err := url.PathUnescape(c.Param("*"))
                if err != nil {
                        return err
                }
                name := filepath.Join(root, path.Clean("/"+p)) // "/"+ for security
                return c.File(name)
        }
        i.GET(prefix, h)
        if prefix == "/" {
                return i.GET(prefix+"*", h)
        }

        return i.GET(prefix+"/*", h)
}
```

The `static` function returns an `*echo.Route` which is a route to a very simple handler. Within the definition above, the handler created first takes the `wildcard` parameter and performs a URL encoding path `unescape` on the parameter. In our case this wildcard parameter is going to be the file name of the asset we wish to serve to the caller. We then generate a file name relative to the root that was defined in the `Static` method call. After we have created a file name from the root of our content directory and the request URI, Echo then performs a `c.File` call to return the file content from the web server. Near the end of this function you can see we are registering this handler for the static assets to the `prefix+"/*"` resource path location.

Clearly, static content delivery builds on top of the file-serving capabilities that are built into Echo. This functionality allows a developer to package up file content and allow that content to be served to callers without having to reimplement a file-serving handler themselves. This feature allows developers to package up static content such as HTML, JavaScript and CSS content within the Go deployment artifact directly.

Template basics

Many times in web applications, there is a need to have dynamic content rendered as well as static content. Typically, the dynamic content supplied to the caller is structured and includes dynamic data. Templates provide the developer with the option to lay out the structure of the response, as well as include syntax to allow for dynamic data. A template in our context is a file that has a preset format which is used as a starting point for a response to a user. Within this section, we will mainly focus on the basics of template syntax using the `html/template` package. Go has a `text/template` package as well as the `html/template` package. The former and later use the same template syntax, but the later provides safety features such as production of HTML output that is safe from code injection. It is important to make sure you use the `html/template` package when rendering HTML so that you can benefit from these safety features.

A template is merely string data which can live as a variable or file content. The following is an example template so we can visualize the syntax of templates using `html/template` which is located at `$GOPATH/src/github.com/PacktPublishing/Echo-Essentials/chapter8/cmd/template-exploration/main.go`:

```
const tmpl = `
<html>
        <head>
                <title>{{.Title}}</title>
        </head>
```

```
            <body>
                    <table>
                            <th>
                                    <td>Reminder Name</td>
                                    <td>Reminder ID</td>
                                    <td>Reminder Due</td>
                            </th>
                            {{ range .Reminders }}
                            <tr>
                                    <td>{{ .Name }}</td>
                                    <td>{{ .ID }}</td>
                                    <td>{{ .Due }}</td>
                            </tr>
                            {{ else }}
                            <tr>
                                    <td colspan=3>No rows!</td>
                            </tr>
                            {{ end }}
            </body>
</html>
```

Within this particular template, we are generating HTML to display a variable number of reminders. We have a document title that is defined as `{{ .Title }}`, and we have a variable, `{{.Reminders}}` that is a list of all of the reminders we are going to render. This syntax may seem strange, with the period prefixing the variable names, but this variable actually represents the current "Context." If you look at the table cell definitions within the `range` we are performing, we are able to specify `{{ .Name }}` because the `{{ .Reminders }}` contains a list of `Reminder` structures that contain an attribute called `Name`. When you are within a `range` block in the template, the "Context" switches to the instance of the structure you get from the range. The following is how we are rendering this template within Go:

```
type Reminder struct {
        ID      uuid.UUID
        Name    string
        Due     time.Time
}

const Week = time.Duration(time.Hour * 24 * 7)

func mustTime(d time.Time, err error) time.Time {
        if err != nil {
                log.Fatalf("failed must condition: %s\n", err.Error())
        }
        return d
```

Providing Templates and Static Content

}

Within the preceding code, we are setting up our `Reminder` structure, as well as creating a week time duration constant and a helper function that will take the tuple result from `time.Parse` and convert it to only the time value. The following is our `main` function where we are setting up two reminders which will be populated in our template from before:

```
func main() {
        reminders := []Reminder{
                Reminder{
                        ID:   uuid.NewV4(),
                        Name: "Oil Change",
                        Due:  time.Now().Add(13 * Week),
                },
                Reminder{
                        ID:   uuid.NewV4(),
                        Name: "Birthday Party",
                        Due:  mustTime(time.Parse("2006-01-02", "2020-01-01")),
                },
        }
```

Now that we have some structure for our template to render, we will parse the template and populate the template with the preceding data. This is accomplished with the `template.New().Parse` functionality in the following example. This will take the template data and parse it into a template. We then populate an anonymous struct with the reminders we created before and run `t.Execute` which actually performs the rendering of the template:

```
        t, err := template.New("reminders").Parse(tmpl)
        if err != nil {
                log.Fatalf("failed to parse template: %s\n", err.Error())
        }

        tmplData := struct {
                Reminders []Reminder
                Title     string
        }{reminders, "Reminders Page"}

        // render the template output based on dynamic data
        err = t.Execute(os.Stdout, tmplData)
        if err != nil {
                log.Fatalf("failed to render template: %s\n", err.Error())
        }
}
```

As you can see in the Go code, we have a structure defined as `Reminder` which includes as attributes, `Name, Due, ID`. We are also creating a new list of these reminder instances. At that point, we generate a new template by calling `template.New("reminders").Parse(tmpl)` that will read in the template string. You could also use `ParseFiles` instead of `Parse`, if you had a file or several you wanted to read in. It is much easier to work with templates as files, as opposed to strings within the application. It is important to note that in a web service it is often best to perform the parsing of the template files at the entry point of the application instead of parsing the templates for every single request. Parsing the templates for every single request would lead to a lot of waste, and should be avoided.

After we have parsed the file, we need to create the data structure that we will feed into the template engine, namely a structure that includes attributes for `Title` and `Reminders` that we reference from within the template. With `tmplData` populated as an anonymous `struct`, we are able to feed the `tmplData` into the template with the `t.Execute` method, which takes in as parameters an `io.Writer` and `interface{}` data. Alternatively, instead of using a `struct` to contain the data for the template it is possible to use a `map` structure instead.

As you can see, within the syntax of the template language, there are conditions such as the `else` on the range. That specifically says if there are no entries within `Reminders`, perform the `else` block.

The following is a high-level outline of the capabilities of the template engine, so that you will be equipped to make use of all of the features included in Go templates:

- `{{/* comment */}}`
  - Comments are discarded and will not show up within the rendered output
  - Comments may be multiple lines, though you are not able to nest comments
- `{{pipeline}}`
  - Think of a pipeline as a contextual denoted variable, such as `{{.Title}}`
  - This will print out the variable using the default output representation

- `{{if pipeline}} T1 {{end}}`
  - Conditional logic is supported, and if the pipeline provided is not empty the internal block will be rendered in the output
  - Empty values include `false`, `0`, nil, or empty array, slice, map, or empty string
- `{{if pipeline}} T1 {{else}} T0 {{end}}`
  - You are able to use conditional `else` statements within templates
- `{{if pipeline}} T1 {{else if pipeline}} T0 {{end}}`
  - You are also able to use conditional `else if` statements
- `{{range pipeline}} T1 {{end}}`
  - You are able to iterate over this pipeline
  - The pipeline must be iterable, array, slice, map, or channel
- `{{range pipeline}} T1 {{else}} T0 {{end}}`
  - If there are no items within the pipeline the `else` block will render
- `{{template "name"}}`
  - The template named `name` will be executed
  - This is primarily used for nested templates
  - The name you specify is the name that was given to the template engine, in our preceding example that would be `reminders`
- `{{template "name" pipeline}}`
  - This template is given a particular pipeline, or context variable which was given to the calling template
- `{{block "name" pipeline}} T1 {{end}}`
  - Block is used to create a "subtemplate" and execute it in place, within a given template
- `{{with pipeline}} T1 {{end}}`
  - `with` is much like the `if` conditional, if the value of the pipeline is empty then no output from the block will be rendered
- `{{with pipeline}} T1 {{else}} T0 {{end}}`
  - `with` also allows for `else` conditions

As noted here, there are significant capabilities within the template engine to create very dynamic content from within templates. It should also be noted that a key use case of templates is not only for web application rendering, but also for email text rendering, or other messaging to users. With all of these capabilities built into the Go standard library, we are able to start looking at the integration with the Echo framework in the next two sections. As we mentioned before the `html/template` package offers a safe way to render HTML outputs, as it will guard against code injection whereas the `text/template` package will not.

Templates within Echo

The Echo framework does provide a facility for custom rendering which is based on the `echo.Renderer` interface. This interface stipulates that implementations have a method `Render` which will perform the rendering of data. With this convention, we are able to take what we learned about Go templates and apply those templates to implement a custom `echo.Renderer` that is capable of rendering HTML templates back to the caller. The following is a very minimal example of an `echo.Renderer` implementation that we have implemented in `$GOPATH/src/github.com/PacktPublishing/Echo-Essentials/chapter8/handlers/reminder.go`:

```go
type CustomTemplate struct {
        *template.Template
}

func (ct *CustomTemplate) Render(w io.Writer, name string, data interface{},
        ctx echo.Context) error {
        return ct.ExecuteTemplate(w, name, data)
}
```

Within this code block, we are creating a `CustomTemplate` structure which is a `template.Template` type. Within the `Render` method, that is required of the `echo.Renderer` interface, we are performing an execute on the template which is named `name` with the pipeline of `data`. Since `template.Template` is capable of handling multiple named templates, we can parse all of our templates into this structure, and reference them by name in our handler code.

Providing Templates and Static Content

For the purposes of our example, I have moved the template we used from the exploration in the previous section into the handler file located at $GOPATH/src/github.com/PacktPublishing/Echo-Essentials/chapter8/handlers/reminder.go, seen as follows:

```
const RemindersTmpl = `
<html>
        <head>
                <title>{{.Title}}</title>
        </head>
        <body>
                <table>
                        <th>
                                <td>Reminder Name</td>
                                <td>Reminder ID</td>
                                <td>Reminder Due</td>
                        </th>
                        {{ range .Reminders }}
                        <tr>
                                <td>{{ .Name }}</td>
                                <td>{{ .ID }}</td>
                                <td>{{ .Due }}</td>
                        </tr>
                        {{ else }}
                        <tr>
                                <td colspan=3>No rows!</td>
                        </tr>
                        {{ end }}
        </body>
</html>
`
```

With this template constant created, and our custom `echo.Renderer` implemented, we are now able to register our custom `echo.Renderer` with Echo itself. This is achieved by the following code in $GOPATH/src/github.com/PacktPublishing/Echo-Essentials/chapter8/cmd/service/main.go:

```
t, err := template.New("reminders").Parse(handlers.RemindersTmpl)
if err != nil {
    panic(err.Error())
}

e.Renderer = &handlers.CustomTemplate{t}
```

Chapter 8

The preceding code first creates a new `html/template.Template` instance named `reminders` and parses our handler's template constant. We then wrap the template in our `handlers.CustomTemplate` structure which has the `echo.Renderer` implementation, and assign our `echo.Echo` instance's `Renderer` attribute to our custom renderer implementation. At this point, we have all of the scaffolding in place to render a template in our handler code, which can be seen in the following code snippet taken from `$GOPATH/src/github.com/PacktPublishing/Echo-Essentials/chapter8/handlers/reminder.go`:

```go
func RenderReminders(c echo.Context) error {
        reminders := []Reminder{
                Reminder{
                        ID:   uuid.NewV4(),
                        Name: "Oil Change",
                        Due:  time.Now().Add(30 * 3 * 24 * time.Hour),
                },
                Reminder{
                        ID:   uuid.NewV4(),
                        Name: "Birthday Party",
                        Due:  mustTime(time.Parse("2006-01-02",
"2020-01-01")),
                },
        }

        tmplData := struct {
                Reminders []Reminder
                Title     string
        }{reminders, "Reminders Page"}

        return c.Render(http.StatusOK, "reminders", tmplData)
}
```

Within our handler, we are creating two reminders, putting these reminders into a template data structure, and then calling `c.Render`. The arguments to `c.Render` are the response status code, then the name of the template to render, and then the template data to populate the template with. When exercised by calling this handler, we get the following populated template rendered back to the caller:

```html
<html>
        <head>
                <title>Reminders Page</title>
        </head>
        <body>
                <table>
                        <th>
                                <td>Reminder Name</td>
```

[113]

Providing Templates and Static Content

```
                                        <td>Reminder ID</td>
                                        <td>Reminder Due</td>
                                </th>
                                <tr>
                                        <td>Oil Change</td>
                                        <td>1c37a3b7-04b6-4920-bd69-
ff591ed13cb8</td>
                                        <td>2018-07-24 09:11:29.038822676 -0400 EDT
m=+7776004.143317695</td>
                                </tr>
                                <tr>
                                        <td>Birthday Party</td>
                                        <td>f729272f-
aecb-4a84-9909-53cbdf5d5af2</td>
                                        <td>2020-01-01 00:00:00 +0000 UTC</td>
                                </tr>
                </body>
</html>
```

As you can see, implementing templates within your Echo project is very simple. There are few moving parts and only one interface to implement (echo.Renderer) in order to produce template-driven renderings to your callers. When married to the functionality of the html/template and text/template capabilities built into the Go standard library, you will be able to produce server-rendered templates very easily. Within the next section, we will discuss how to reach back into Echo from templates.

Calling Echo from templates

There are times when it is handy to access functionality and methods of the web framework from within a template being rendered. A primary use case of this is to figure out reverse URLs for rendering links within a page. Luckily, due to the fact that Go allows for functions as variables, we are able to do this quite easily. The first thing we have to do is formalize the tmplData anonymous struct to include a method that we would want to call from within the template. Go's template library supports execution of methods by name which allows us to call methods off of the data struct that is passed into the execute. With this in mind, we will expose a Reverse function in our template data struct in which we can pass in Echo's Reverse function. The following code is located at $GOPATH/src/github.com/PacktPublishing/Echo-Essentials/chapter8/handlers/reminder.go:

```
type TmplData struct {
        Reminders []Reminder
        Title     string
```

```
                rev         func(name string, params ...interface{}) string
}

func (td TmplData) Reverse(name string, params ...interface{}) string {
        return td.rev(name, params...)
}
```

We are able to take this type now and populate it with any reverse function we want as seen here:

```
        data := TmplData{reminders, "Reminders Page", c.Echo().Reverse}
        return c.Render(http.StatusOK, "reminders", data)
```

Now that we have our template being rendered with a Reverse method built into the template data structure we can use this new functionality to have our templates figure out URL link reversals. This is extremely beneficial when you need to have links generated from within a template. In order to perform this we need to name the routes we wish to have URL reversals for explicitly as shown below in `cmd/service/main.go`

```
        e.POST("/login", handlers.Login).Name = "login"
```

After we have this route name in place, we need to update our template to add a link to the `login` named route. Below is the modified rendered template, which includes a line specifying that we would like to have a `login` link, and use the `Reverse` template data method we have created previously to render this link to the `/login` route:

```
<html>
        <head>
                <title>{{.Title}}</title>
        </head>
        <body>
          <a href={{ .Reverse "login" }}>Login</a>
                <table>
                        <th>
                                <td>Reminder Name</td>
                                <td>Reminder ID</td>
                                <td>Reminder Due</td>
                        </th>
                        {{ range .Reminders }}
                        <tr>
                                <td>{{ .Name }}</td>
                                <td>{{ .ID }}</td>
                                <td>{{ .Due }}</td>
                        </tr>
                        {{ else }}
                        <tr>
```

Providing Templates and Static Content

```
                                <td colspan=3>No rows!</td>
                        </tr>
                        {{ end }}
        </body>
</html>
```

When this template is rendered the `TmplData.Reverse` method is called with the parameter `"login"` which in turn calls our Echo instance's `Reverse` function. This will look up a route with a name `login` and return the full route associated. Following is the rendered content of the template:

```
<html>
        <head>
                <title>Reminders Page</title>
        </head>
        <body>
                <a href=/login>Login</a>
                <table>
                        <th>
                                <td>Reminder Name</td>
                                <td>Reminder ID</td>
                                <td>Reminder Due</td>
                        </th>
                        <tr>
                                <td>Oil Change</td>
                                <td>7edc58cf-bd3f-48cb-b741-
b2cafb106943</td>
                                <td>2018-08-12 22:49:02.562939274 -0400 EDT
m=+7776002.527394939</td>
                        </tr>
                        <tr>
                                <td>Birthday Party</td>
                                <td>b6b0da75-bbd5-4d61-9090-
c88b9ca0dcec</td>
                                <td>2020-01-01 00:00:00 +0000 UTC</td>
                        </tr>
        </body>
</html>
```

As you can see, we have a new line in our template rendered output that shows `<a href=/login>Login</a>` which is a link to the login route. This very simple change has allowed us to inject the Echo instance's `Reverse` method into our template effectively. It is fairly trivial to add more functionality to this `TmplData` structure to allow for your templates to have access to any aspect of your application. This sort of flexibility will allow you to quickly create server-side rendered templates that make your application more dynamic and flexible.

Summary

As with any fully rounded web application framework, the developer should have the ability to serve static and dynamic assets. With Echo, you have the ability to serve static content with the `Static` Echo instance method, as well as the ability to serve individual files with the `File` Echo instance method.

Often, it is not enough merely to serve static content. Echo also provides the ability to serve dynamic templates, which can be populated with dynamic data, as shown in this chapter. Within this chapter, we have shown not only how to render dynamic data from templates, but also how to call back into Echo from within the templates themselves.

Other Books You May Enjoy

If you enjoyed this book, you may be interested in these other books by Packt:

Distributed Computing with Go
V.N. Nikhil Anurag

ISBN: 978-1-78712-538-4

- Gain proficiency with concurrency and parallelism in Go
- Learn how to test your application using Go's standard library
- Learn industry best practices with technologies such as REST, OpenAPI, Docker, and so on
- Design and build a distributed search engine
- Learn strategies on how to design a system for web scale

Go Web Development Cookbook
Arpit Aggarwal

ISBN: 978-1-78728-674-0

- Create a simple HTTP and TCP web server and understand how it works
- Explore record in a MySQL and MongoDB database
- Write and consume RESTful web service in Go
- Invent microservices in Go using Micro – a microservice toolkit
- Create and Deploy the Beego application with Nginx
- Deploy Go web application and Docker containers on an AWS EC2 instance

Leave a review - let other readers know what you think

Please share your thoughts on this book with others by leaving a review on the site that you bought it from. If you purchased the book from Amazon, please leave us an honest review on this book's Amazon page. This is vital so that other potential readers can see and use your unbiased opinion to make purchasing decisions, we can understand what our customers think about our products, and our authors can see your feedback on the title that they have worked with Packt to create. It will only take a few minutes of your time, but is valuable to other potential customers, our authors, and Packt. Thank you!

Index

A
application panics
  handling 87, 88

B
basic handler routing 36
behavior testing 91
benchmark testing 90

C
constants, Go net/http package
  reference 9
context mapping
  requesting, globally 65, 66
context
  hiding, within request 67
  managing 64, 65
  post Go 1.7 68
custom middleware
  about 32
  creating 57, 58

D
dependency management 26

E
Echo routing
  working 38, 39, 40
echo.Context interface
  methods 68, 69
echo.Response 76, 78
Echo
  calling, from templates 114, 116
  code organization 20
  example project implementation 24, 25
  project setup 20
  setting up 16, 17
environment
  setting up 14
error handling 85, 86, 87

F
framework
  need for 14

G
Go HTTP handlers 12
Go HTTP web server 13
Gorilla
  reference 65
group routing 40, 42

H
handler code 91, 93, 95
handler function type 66, 67
handlers 28, 30
HTTP request
  about 9
  Request HTTP Version (RFC-7230 2.6) 9
  Request Method (RFC-7231 4.3; RFC-5789 2) 9
  Request Target (RFC-7230 5.3) 9
HTTP response
  about 11
  HTTP-Version (RFC-7230 2.6) 11
  reason-phrase 11
  Status-Code (RFC-7231 6) 11
http.Request type
  reference 9
http.ResponseWriter type
  reference 11
Hypertext Transport Protocol (HTTP)

    basics 8

I

integration testing 91, 98

J

JSON Web Token (JWT) 59

L

labstack/gommon/log logger
   reference 81
log levels 83, 84
Logger interface 81, 82
logger middleware 84
logging 80

M

middleware chaining 53, 55
middleware processing
  basics 50, 51, 52, 53
middleware
  about 31
  custom middleware 32
  in example application 59, 60
monkey patching
  reference 96
MSI Installer for Go
  download link 15

N

net/url package
  reference 9

R

rendering
  capabilities 32, 33
request binding 70, 71, 72, 74
request
  context, hiding within 67
response rendering 75

  router implementation
    considerations 42, 43
routes
  adding 36, 38
routing
  about 27, 28
  working 44

S

security testing 91
static files
  serving 104, 105, 106

T

template
  basics 106, 108, 109, 111
  Echo, calling from 114, 116
  implementing, within Echo 111, 113
testing
  about 90
  behavior testing 91
  benchmark testing 90
  integration testing 91
  security testing 91
  unit testing 90
Transport Layer Security (TLS) 13

U

Unified Resource Locator (URL) 9
Uniform Resource Identifier (URI) 9
unit testing 90
unit testing middleware 91, 93, 95

V

Vestigo URL Router
  reference 67

W

web applications
  benchmark testing 97

Printed in Poland
by Amazon Fulfillment
Poland Sp. z o.o., Wrocław

31948926R00078